Quick
& Easy

Beaded

Jewelry

Elizabeth Gourley
Ellen Talbott

Published by

krause
publications

700 East State Street • Iola, WI 54990-0001
715/445-2214 • FAX: 715/445-4087   www.krause.com

Please call or write for our free catalog of publications. To place an order or obtain a free catalog, please call (800) 258-0929, or please use our regular business telephone: (715) 445-2214.

Library of Congress Catalog Number: 2002105086
ISBN: 0-87349-377-X

Dedication

This book is dedicated to our loving families: Mike, Amy, Greg, Alan, Walter, and George.

Acknowledgments

We would like to thank Amy Tincher-Durik for believing in our ideas and Christine Townsend for all her hard work and great editing. Thanks also to Donna Mummery, the designer of this book. We would like to thank our friend, Jane Davis, who, with all her creative energy, gives us the extra little push and motivation it takes to go ahead and get off the couch and write a book. And we can't forget to thank our families for being there for us.

Photographs by Ellen Talbott

Table of Contents

Chapter Three 31

Chapter Four 55

Chapter Five 63

Chapter Six 110

Introduction: Tools, Thread and Wires, Findings

To bead or not to bead—that is the question—but only if you've never beaded before. Once you start beading, you can't stop: You'll never entertain the *thought* of whether to bead or not—you'll just *bead*! That's how easily beading can become an enjoyable part of life.

Beads and making beaded adornment have been around for so long, from the beginning of mankind, that by now the need for beads and beading is instinctive—nearly (in our opinion) as basic as the need for food and shelter. We must warn you: A full-blown case of "bead addiction" can turn your world upside down … you may find (like we did) that since you must bead, the dust in your home accumulates and your golf clubs never see the light of day. You may end up spending every spare minute (and some minutes you perhaps shouldn't spare!) beading.

In order to help relieve this problem, we have written this book. The thirty projects can be quickly and easily finished, leaving us with more time for the rest of the things in our lives. Each sophisticated piece comes with instructions for a matching set. In just a few hours of work, you will have beautiful jewelry, from casual to evening wear, to show off—or give as gifts—to all your friends and family members … and still get that dusting done.

If you've never beaded before, this book will offer help to you, too. One look at the things you can do with a few beads and a small amount of effort, and the "to bead or not to bead" question will be quickly answered: To bead is the only way to be!

We've been beading for many years. Ellen started out collecting beadwork from her forays into the Southwest, picking up anything beaded by Native Americans. She also collects African beadwork. Finally, she decided to try beading for herself and hasn't stopped!

Liz was inspired to bead by her friend, Kari, who made beaded earrings. One day they went to the bead store together. Oh! So many beautiful beads and so little time! The ideas of what one could make with beads filled Liz's head to overflowing and all her spare time is spent buying beads, looking at beads and, of course, *beading*.

So it is our love of beads that led us to create this book in the hopes of sharing with others. Use this book as a resource guide: Make the projects, get inspired, and most of all have fun! Be creative! Feel free to change the colors of the projects or to use your favorite beads or findings in place of the ones used in this book.

If you have trouble finding supplies, we have provided a resource list at the back of the book.

Abbreviations Used in This Book
PNT – *Pass the needle through*
PNBT – *Pass the needle back through*
BT – *Back through*

TOOLS

The tools needed for making beaded jewelry are fairly basic and inexpensive. Jewelry makers' pliers and wire cutters are essential tools of the trade, along with beading needles, knotting tweezers, scissors, bead boards, and glue.

PLIERS

Round-Nose Pliers
These pliers have tapering cylindrical ends perfect for making loops in wire or on head pins and eye pins. They can be used to hold small findings and are also useful for closing the loops on bead tips.

Chain-Nose Pliers
These versatile pliers have tapered half-round ends. They are good for gripping, crimping, wire wrapping, opening and closing jump rings, and squeezing bead tips closed.

Flat-Nose Pliers
The flat-nose pliers have flat, straight ends that don't taper. The inside surface is smooth and won't make marks on the wire or findings. Use them to bend wire at angles, to open and close jump rings, and to squeeze bead tips closed.

These are the three basic "you must have" pliers. The following are more specialized pliers that you might like to have to make things a little easier.

Bent Chain-Nose Pliers
These pliers are like chain-nose pliers, except the ends are curved at about a thirty-degree angle. They are good for getting into hard-to-reach places, gripping, and wire wrapping.

Crimping Pliers
These pliers are used for only one thing, but they are very good at what they do. Crimping pliers have two indentions on their inside surfaces. The one closest to the handle is the crimper, which makes a dimple in the crimp bead. The indention closest to the tip of the

pliers is called the rounder and this finishes off the crimp by squeezing the crimp bead into a round shape.

Split-Ring Pliers

These pliers have thin, tapering ends. The tip of one of the ends is bent inward at a sharp angle. They are used to open split rings of all sizes for ease in attaching them to other split rings or other findings.

Loop-Closing Pliers

These pliers are useful for closing jump rings or chain links without marking the surface of the metal. The inside surfaces of the pliers are smooth and have slots for holding the links or the jump rings.

Wire-Looping or Coil Pliers

These pliers have one smooth flat end and one similar to round-nose pliers, only with three tiers along its length. This is used for making wire coils or wire loops that are consistent in size. You can make three different sizes with them.

Rosary Pliers

Rosary pliers are a combination round-nose pliers and side wire cutters.

WIRE CUTTERS

There are two basic kinds of wire cutters: The side cutter and the end, or flush cutter. The side cutter has blades on the inside surfaces of the jaws and is good for cutting wire or tiger tail. The flush cutter has the blades on the tips of the jaws and is good for cutting things flush, so no wire tail remains.

Specialized cutters, of the side-cutter variety, are also made for tiger tail and stretchy cord.

SCISSORS

Scissors are used to cut beading thread. We like to use embroidery scissors because their slender, sharp ends makes cutting the thread close to the bead easier. There is also a thread cutter that has no finger holes, has very sharp edges, and works well for snipping thread or cord.

KNOTTING TWEEZERS

Knotting tweezers are not only good for making knots, but also are handy to have about for picking up or holding small beads or findings. They have sharp precision tips and slender jaws.

Clockwise from the center: Knotting tweezers, embroidery scissors, crimp pliers, bent chain-nose pliers, flush wire cutters, side wire cutters, rosary pliers, round-nose pliers, chain-nose pliers and flat-nose pliers.

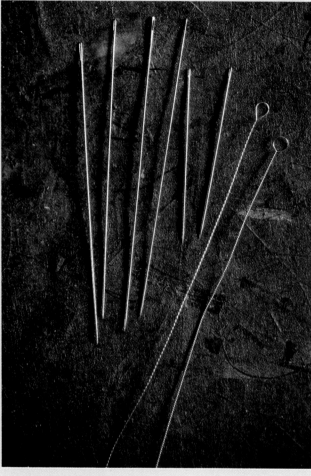

An assortment of beading needles.

NEEDLES

There are three basic kinds of beading needles: big-eye needles, twisted wire needles, and beading needles.

Beading Needles

Beading needles have sharp ends and are shaped like sewing needles, but they are much thinner, have smaller eyes and don't taper to the end. The eyes are small enough to fit through tiny bead holes. Beading needles come in several sizes based on their length and thickness. The lengths are approximately 1-1/4", 2", and 3". The 3" needles are used mostly for bead-loom work. The most popular thickness of beading needles are from #10s (thick) to #15s (very thin). In this book, we used primarily #11s and #12s. These two sizes fit well in size 11° seed beads.

Twisted Wire Beading Needles

These needles are useful for larger thread or cord that won't fit through the eye of a beading needle. They are made of a length of wire twisted back on itself, so they don't have a sharp point. The eye is a large loop that collapses as it goes through the bead. Twisted needles come in four sizes: light, light-medium, medium-heavy, and heavy.

Big-Eye Needles

Big-eye needles have one large eye that runs the length of the needle. Only the two ends of the needle are attached. These needles have sharp points. They are used for easy threading no matter how thin or thick the thread.

JEWELRY MAKERS' BEAD BOARDS

Bead Boards

Bead boards are used to design and measure your bead strands before you string them. They are made of wood, plastic, or flocked plastic. They usually have inch markings along the strand indentions and have space for one to five strands, depending on the size of the board.

Beading Trays

Beading trays are good for use with seed beads. You can keep the different color seed beads you might need for a project separated and the beads are spread out for ease in picking them up. Some come with lids for storage and travel.

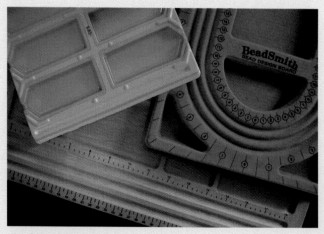

Bead boards and trays.

GLUE

Glue is an essential tool in making beaded jewelry, from securing knots to attaching beads to findings. You can find many bonding-cement type glues at craft or bead stores. The best glues will adhere almost any surfaces and, when dry, will be clear, flexible, and waterproof.

THREADS AND WIRES

There are many different materials used to string beads together. In fact, you can use virtually whatever fits through the beads you want to use. However, there are several common threads and wires used in the beading world today.

THREAD

Nylon Beading Thread or Nymo™

Nymo (nylon monofilament) looks like dental floss, and is great for using with seed beads and for making bead strands. It comes in black and white plus a variety of other colors. Thinnest is size 000, medium-thin is size 0 or A, size B is medium, D is medium-thick and sizes E, F, FF, and FFF are thickest, respectively.

Silamide

This is a type of twisted nylon thread that comes in sizes A or 0. This thread is not as stiff as Nymo. It is good for seed beads or bead strands.

Kevlar™

Kevlar is another seed bead thread that is very strong, since it is made from the same material as bulletproof vests. It comes in black or a yellowish off-white color.

Silk or Nylon Twisted Thread

This thread is used for knotting. It most often comes on cards, but you can get it on spools. The sizes on cards are numbered, the thinnest being 0 and the thickest being 16. Some brands use the alphabet sizing with 00 being thinnest, C and D being medium weight and FFF the thickest.

Stretchy Cord

Stretchy cord is elastic cord used most often for bracelets and other jewelry. It comes in several diameters. Pick the one that fits through your beads the best. The thin size can fit through seed bead holes. Thinnest is size .5mm and 2mm is the thickest. It comes in several colors, but the most popular is clear.

Stretchy Floss

There is also stretchy floss that looks similar to Nymo thread, but it is elastic. This type is harder to find and tends to fray, but is easier to knot than the stretchy cord.

Satin Cord

Satin cord is great for knotting or stringing a few larger beads. It comes in many colors and three main thicknesses: 1mm, 1.5mm and 2mm. Cotton or hemp cord is also made to be used with beads.

Leather or Imitation Leather Cord

Leather or imitation leather cord works great with large-holed beads. It comes in sizes from .5mm to 3mm.

A variety of threads and cord.

Beading wire.

WIRE

Beading Wire or Tiger Tail

Beading wire is made of several thin wires twisted together and then covered with nylon. It comes in several sizes: .012 and .014 are thin, .018 and .019 are medium, .022 and .024 medium-thick, .026 thick. Tiger tail is good for stranding and for beads with sharp edges that might cut through other beading threads. Crimp beads are used with tiger tail.

Memory Wire

Memory wire is a stiff, pre-coiled wire that will return to its original shape after being pulled apart. It is made in three coil sizes: One to use for necklaces, one for bracelets and one small one that is ring sized. It usually comes in packages with twelve loops of wire that must be cut to one loop for necklaces or from one to four for bracelets and rings. Memory wire is too stiff for jewelry pliers, so you have to use regular pliers when making loops on the ends.

Wire for Jewelry Making

Wire comes in gold or silver tone metal, aluminum, or precious metal (gold-filled, 14k or 18k gold and sterling silver). Wire known as niobium comes in many different colors. Beading wire is sized by gauges with 8 gauge being thickest and 34 being thinnest.

Sizes 18-, 20-, 22-, 24-, 26-, and 28-gauge round wires are the most popular sizes for beadwork. Ultra thin size 34 is great for seed beads. Wire also comes in square, half-round, and triangle shapes. Their gauges are also numbered with the higher the number the smaller the diameter and the lower the number the bigger the diameter. These wires are good for wire wrapping.

FINDINGS

Findings are used to put beads, thread and/or wire together to make personal adornment. They are a very important part of jewelry making. Findings include, but are not limited to: clasps, bead tips or knot covers, head pins, eye pins, jump rings, split-rings, bullion or French wire, cord tips, crimp beads, bails or triangles, cones, bell caps, bead caps, spacer bars, barrette backs, earring wires and posts, pin backs, neckwires and chains.

These findings can be found in precious metal (14k or 18k gold, sterling silver), titanium, gold plated or silver plated, gold filled, surgical steel (ear wires and studs mostly), nickel-plated, brass, copper and gold tone or silver tone metal. You can even find jump rings, eye pins, head pins, and a few other findings in red, pink, blue, purple, green, and yellow.

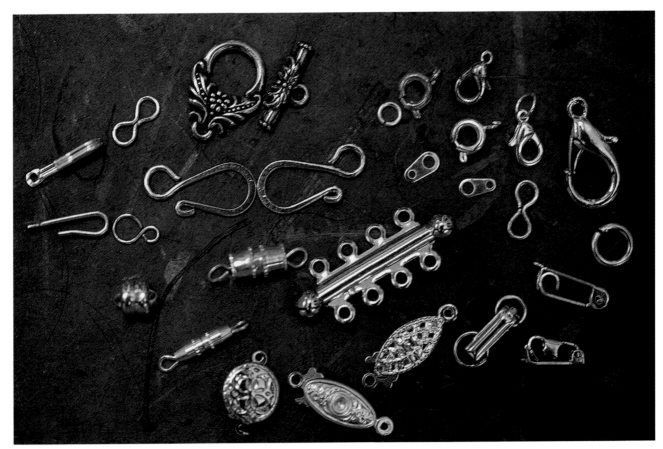

Clasps. Counterclockwise from 11:00 o'clock: Fancy toggle clasp, hook and eye clasps, barrel clasp, magnetic clasp, torpedo clasp, insert-style clasp, fishhook clasp, tube clasp, fold-over clasps, lobster clasps and spring ring clasps.

CLASPS

Clasps are used to hook necklace, bracelet or anklet ends together. There are many types of clasps, the most common ones being the spring ring, fishhook, lobster-claw, hook and eye, barrel, magnetic, fold-over, two-to-five-strand tube, bar and ring or toggle, and insert-style.

Spring Ring Clasp

Spring rings are circular in shape, and you need either a jump ring or a chain tab to complete the clasp. To open a spring ring, you press down on the push tab. It has a spring mechanism so that once the tab is released the clasp automatically closes.

Fishhook Clasp

Fishhook clasps are made with security in mind. One end of the clasp is shaped like a fishhook. The hook side is inserted into the other end of the clasp, over a little bar. Then the fishhook side is pushed until it snaps shut. Even if this clasp were to pop open, the fishhook would still be attached because of the little bar.

Lobster Claw Clasp

These clasps are similar to spring rings in that they have a push tab to open them, and they close automatically when the push tab is released. The other end of the clasp can be a jump ring or a chain tab.

Hook and Eye Clasp

Hook and eye clasps are very basic clasps comprised of a hook and a double ring end or a jump ring end. They are easy to use: Simply place the hook into the ring. Some hook and eye clasps are in an "S" shape.

Barrel Clasps

Barrel clasps look like little barrels when closed. They are screwed open and closed. Torpedo clasps are similar to barrel clasps, but they are thinner.

Magnetic Clasps

These clasps are simply two very small but powerful magnets set inside round clasps that have one smooth side and one side with a loop for connecting the jewelry strand. The two smooth sides are attracted to each other. Magnetic clasps are easy to open and close.

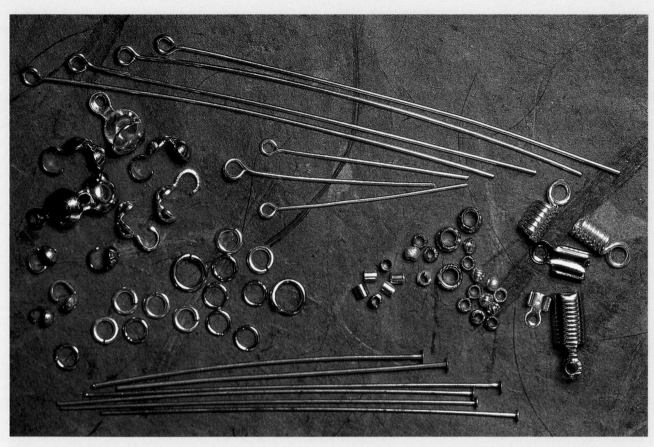

Findings. Counterclockwise from the top: Eye pins, bead tips, jump rings, head pins, tube crimps, crimp beads, cord tips, and cord coils.

Fold-Over Clasps

Fold-over clasps are the kind found on many watches or bracelets. The fold-over side goes into the bar side and folds over the bar and clips onto itself.

Tube or Slide Lock Clasps

Tube or slide lock bars are clasps that have from two-to-five loops on one side of both ends to attach separate strands. To close the clasp, one side slides up and over the other side.

Toggle Clasps or Bar and Ring Clasps

This clasp consists of a large ring and a bar. The bar is longer than the diameter of the ring. Slip the bar into the ring by holding the bar in a vertical position. Then let go of the bar and it will go back to its horizontal position and be secure on the other side of the ring.

Insert-Style Clasps

These clasps are usually fancy clasps that come in different shapes. Some are round, some are square, and some are the shapes of animals or hearts. The smaller end is inserted into the larger end and snapped closed. They are similar to a fishhook clasp without the little bar.

BEAD TIPS OR KNOT COVERS

Bead tips are used to hide knots at the ends of necklaces and bracelets and have a loop at one end to attach the clasp to. There are three kinds of bead tips: The standard, the side-clamp-on and the bottom-clamp-on style. The standard style consists of a little cup to hold the knot and a hole in the bottom for the thread to go through and a loop at the top to attach the clasp. The loop is closed with round-nose pliers. The side-clamp-on style has its hinge on the side and two little cups that, when squeezed together, go over the end knot. There is a circular loop on the top for attaching the clasp. The bottom-clamp-on style is sometimes called a clamshell. It also has two little cups that, when squeezed together, cover up the knot; however, its hinge is on the bottom and has a hole in it for the thread to go through. On the top of one of the little cups is a loop for attaching the clasp. Use round-nose pliers to close the loop around the

Findings. Counterclockwise from the upper right corner: Cones, fancy separators, bead caps, bails, cord caps and, in the middle, bell caps.

clasp. We prefer the bottom-clamp-on or clamshell type bead tip—it covers the knot completely and seems the most secure of the three.

JUMP RINGS & SPLIT RINGS

Jump rings are rings of wire that are round or oval, soldered or non-soldered. They are sized by the diameter and run from 2mm all the way up to 12mm. They are used for joining and/or attaching clasps, chains, eye pins, head pins, and wire loops. They join dangles to earrings or necklaces and combine beads with wire and/or chains. Split rings are rings of doubled wire and are used like jump rings. They come in a wide variety of sizes from 5mm to 28mm.

CRIMP BEADS

These beads are used instead of knots on beading wire such as tiger tail. They secure the ends and help make the loop used to attach clasps. They come in sizes 2mm, 3mm, and 4mm. Crimp beads can't be used with thread or cord, because when you crimp them tight, it might cut the thread or cord. You can also use crimp tubes in the same manner as crimp beads.

HEAD PINS AND EYE PINS

These findings are very important in beaded jewelry making. They are used to make dangles, earrings and bead links. Head pins are lengths of wire with a round pinhead on one end and eye pins are lengths of wire with a round loop at one end. They are measured by thickness and length. The thickness is measured in inches with .020" being the thinnest and .029" the thickest. The shortest length is 1/2" and the longest is 4" long. Some head pins have flattened paddle-type heads instead of round heads.

CORD TIPS

Cord tips are used with cord larger than 2mm. There are two kinds of cord tip. The cord crimp has a loop for attaching the clasp and flaps that are folded over the cord end and squeezed tight. It also has a sharp arrowhead-shaped piece of metal sticking out of the bottom middle of the tip; this grabs the cord and holds it tight. The other kind of cord tip is basically a cup with a loop on one end. The cord is glued into the cup.

CORD COILS

These are a form of cord crimp. A cord coil is a length of coiled wire that has a loop on one end for attaching the clasp. It is slipped onto the end of the cord and then the coil farthest from the looped end is crimped tight.

CONES

A cone is used in multi-strand jewelry to help hide the ends of all the strands. Cones have a wide mouth and a smaller hole on the other end.

CORD CAPS

Cord caps are similar to cones; they look like cups with holes on the bottom. They are used for multiple strand jewelry to hide the knots.

BEAD CAPS

A bead cap is a little metal cup with a hole in the bottom which is strung on next to a bead so it fits over the bead like a cap. You can have one bead cap per bead or two, one on each end of the bead.

BELL CAPS

Bell caps are used to make any object that doesn't have a hole in it into a bead by giving it a hole without drilling. They are caps with prongs and a loop on the top. Bend the prongs around the object and glue in place. Bell caps come in small sizes and large sizes with four or seven prongs. Use whatever size fits the object the best.

BULLION OR FRENCH WIRE

Bullion is made up of coils of thin wire, and is used to reinforce the section of beading cord or thread that is threaded through the clasp. It comes in long lengths that must be cut to size.

BAILS OR TRIANGLES

These findings are used to make pendants. Some kinds are glued to the bead or stone. Others have prongs that fit into the hole of the pendant. Triangles are used when the hole of the pendant is too far down on the bead or the pendant is too thick to use a jump ring.

SPACER BARS

Spacer bars are used on multi-strand necklaces or bracelets. They are threaded on at intervals along the necklace or bracelet to keep the strands equidistant from each other. They come in several sizes with holes to accommodate from two to ten strands. They can be plain or fancy.

NECK WIRES

These are rigid rings of wire that fit around your neck. They come with a threaded-ball-screw clasp. Most neck wires are fairly thick, so you must use large-holed beads. They are usually 16" in diameter.

EAR WIRES

Ear wires are meant for pierced ears. Clips and screw-ons are for non-pierced ears. There are five main types of ear wires for pierced ears: Fishhook, kidney-shaped, lever-back, hoops, and posts or studs. They come in several wire weights from 24-gauge (lightest) to 20-gauge (heaviest). Fishhook ear wires are basically just that, hooks that fit into your ears. They have a small loop on the front end so you can add the beaded designs or dangles. A kidney ear wire is a wire bent into a kidney shape with a little hook bent into the bottom end of the wire that the top wire end fits into to close the earring. They also have a dip in the front

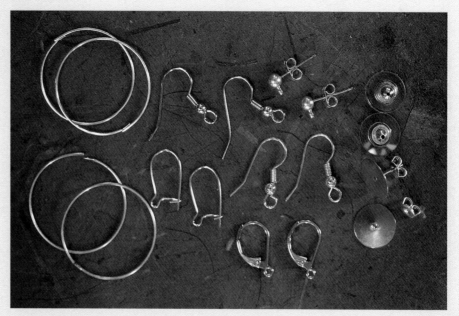

Ear wires. Counterclockwise from the upper left corner: Silver hoops, gold hoops, kidney wires, lever backs, flat pad studs, comfort clutch earring backs, drop studs, and fishhooks.

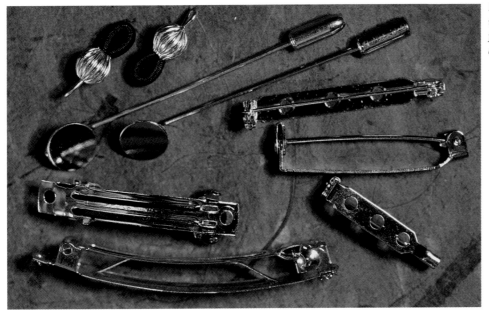

end of the wire to use to add the dangles, etc. A lever-back ear wire has a sophisticated hinge and a lever on the back of the ear wire that can be snapped open and closed. It also has a loop on the front for adding the beads. A hoop earring wire can be used as a plain earring or you can liven it up with beads. Post or stud ear wires come in two forms. The flat pad ear studs or drop ear studs. The flat pad ear studs have a flat metal surface on the front of the stud to use as a place to glue the beadwork. Drop ear studs have a small loop on the front to use to attach dangles, etc.

Pin Backs

These are used for making pins or broaches. They come with flat round, oval or rectangle fronts where you can glue almost anything to make into a pin. They also come with a rectangle front that has holes in it so you can glue or sew whatever you are using to make a pin. They come in various lengths from 3/4" to 2".

Barrette Backs

Barrette backs are very similar to pin backs. They are found in longer lengths than the pin backs and are used to hold hair.

Eyeglass Chain Findings

These findings are used to make eyeglass chains and have loops at either end, one loop to attach to the eyeglasses and one to attach to the beads.

Chain

Chains come in bulk or precut lengths in many link styles. Two basic link styles are the cable chain and the figaro chain. Each of these styles comes in fancy variations and different weights, from light chain (.4gms) to heavy chain (23gms).

Cable chain

Figaro chain

BEADS

Once upon a time, long, long ago, one of our ancient predecessors poked a hole in a bone or a seed or a stone, and lo! The beloved bead was born.

Anything with a hole through it can be considered a bead. Beads are made from many different things in many different shapes and sizes ... there are metal beads, novelty beads, pressed glass beads, lampwork beads, pearl beads, semi-precious stone and gemstone beads, crystal beads, faceted glass beads, wood beads, horn beads, bone beads, shell beads, seeds as beads, cloisonné beads, trade beads, ceramic beads, drop beads, seed beads, pony beads, Japanese tubular beads, white heart beads, bugle beads, druk beads, rondelles, cane glass beads, cat's eye fiber optic beads, miracle beads, hex beads, triangle beads, square beads, acrylic and plastic beads, polymer clay beads, and heishe beads—and there are many more types of beads.

Beads. Counterclockwise from the upper left corner: An assortment of seed beads, crystal beads, bugle beads, faceted glass beads, and cathedral beads.

Counterclockwise from the upper left corner: Stone beads, shell beads, wood beads, seeds as beads, metal beads, bone beads, and horn beads.

Beads. Counterclockwise from the upper left corner: Lampwork beads, druk beads, cat's eye beads, novelty beads, and pressed glass beads.

Jewelry

Standards

and

Techniques

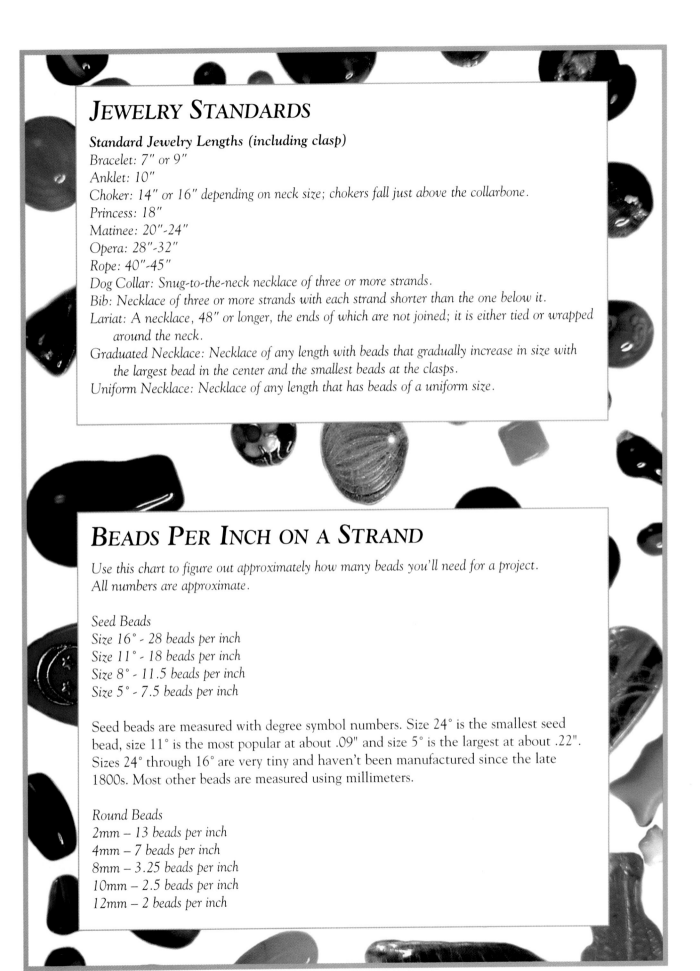

JEWELRY STANDARDS

Standard Jewelry Lengths (including clasp)

Bracelet: 7" or 9"

Anklet: 10"

Choker: 14" or 16" depending on neck size; chokers fall just above the collarbone.

Princess: 18"

Matinee: 20"-24"

Opera: 28"-32"

Rope: 40"-45"

Dog Collar: Snug-to-the-neck necklace of three or more strands.

Bib: Necklace of three or more strands with each strand shorter than the one below it.

Lariat: A necklace, 48" or longer, the ends of which are not joined; it is either tied or wrapped around the neck.

Graduated Necklace: Necklace of any length with beads that gradually increase in size with the largest bead in the center and the smallest beads at the clasps.

Uniform Necklace: Necklace of any length that has beads of a uniform size.

BEADS PER INCH ON A STRAND

Use this chart to figure out approximately how many beads you'll need for a project. All numbers are approximate.

Seed Beads

Size 16° - 28 beads per inch

Size 11° - 18 beads per inch

Size 8° - 11.5 beads per inch

Size 5° - 7.5 beads per inch

Seed beads are measured with degree symbol numbers. Size 24° is the smallest seed bead, size 11° is the most popular at about .09" and size 5° is the largest at about .22". Sizes 24° through 16° are very tiny and haven't been manufactured since the late 1800s. Most other beads are measured using millimeters.

Round Beads

2mm – 13 beads per inch

4mm – 7 beads per inch

8mm – 3.25 beads per inch

10mm – 2.5 beads per inch

12mm – 2 beads per inch

TECHNIQUES

How to Attach a Clasp Using Thread

Attaching a clasp using beading thread is quite simple. Make sure to leave a fairly long tail on both ends of the piece. String one end of a clasp onto one end of the thread. Wrap thread around the clasp loop several times by passing thread through the loop several times, and pull tight. Tie a double-half hitch knot right below the clasp loop (fig. 1). Repeat one or two times. Then hide the tail through a few beads. For extra security, tie another overhand knot, if the bead holes are big enough to hide the knot (fig. 2). Cut off the excess thread. Place a dab of glue on the first knot to secure it. Let dry. Using the tail of thread on the other end of the piece, repeat the instructions.

clasp loop onto the wire, then pass the wire back through the crimp bead, pulling tight so that there is just a small loop between the crimp bead and the clasp loop (fig. 1). Crush the crimp bead, first with the crimping hole of the crimping pliers (fig. 2) and then finish it off by squeezing the dimpled crimp bead with the rounding hole of the pliers (fig. 3). When crimping, try to keep the wires separated so that one is caught on one side of the dimple and one on the other side. Cut the excess wire about 1/2" from the crimp bead. String your beads making sure the first few beads go over both strands of wire to hide the excess tail. When you finish stringing on the beads, string on one crimp bead, and then the other end of the clasp. Pass the wire back through the crimp bead

Figure 1

Figure 2

How to Attach a Clasp Using Crimp Beads and Tiger Tail

Attaching a clasp using crimp beads is one of the easiest ways of attaching a clasp. Attach one end of the clasp before you start stringing your beads. Here's how to do it: On the length of tiger tail or beading wire, string one crimp bead (make sure that if you are using thin beading wire you use a smaller crimp bead and if you are using thicker wire or more than one strand of wire use the larger diameter crimp bead). Slip the

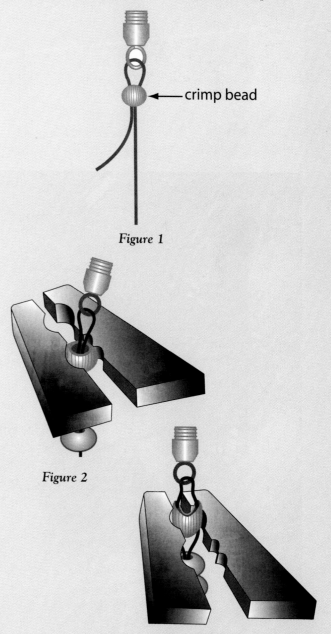

Figure 1

Figure 2

Figure 3

and pull tight, making sure the beads are tight against the crimp bead and clasp end. Then squeeze the crimp bead with crimp pliers. Pass the tail end of the wire back through several beads then cut the excess.

How to Attach a Clasp Using Bead Tips (Bottom Clamp-On or Clamshell-Type Bead Tips)

There are several ways to attach a bead tip to the thread. If you are using thick thread or multiple threads, you can attach a bead tip by tying a knot. First string on a bead tip then tie an overhand knot or two as tightly into the bead tip as possible (fig. 1). If you have multiple threads, you may tie a square knot. Cut excess thread and place a drop of glue onto the knot. Then using pliers (flat-nose or chain-nose), squeeze the bead tip closed over the knot. When the beading thread is thin and the knot or knots would slip right out of the bead tip, you may use a seed bead to help hold the thread in the bead tip. First, string a clamshell bead tip onto the thread then string a seed bead. Size 11° seed beads work well. Pass the needle through the bead again then tie an overhand knot. Repeat one or two times. Make sure the bead is pulled tightly inside the two cups of the bead tip (fig. 2). Cut excess thread from the knot. Place a dab of glue over the bead and the knot and squeeze the bead

tip cups shut over the knot and the bead using chain-nose or flat-nose pliers. If you have two or more thin threads, you may tie the thread ends together over the bead using a square knot (fig. 3). To attach a clasp to the bead tip, slip the clasp onto the hook on the top of the bead tip (fig. 4). Close the bead tip hook using round-nose pliers and a turning motion (fig. 5). Repeat on the other end of the piece.

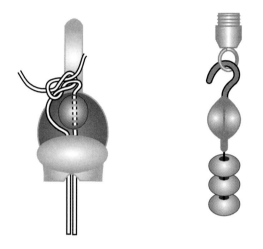

Figure 3   *Figure 4*

Figure 5

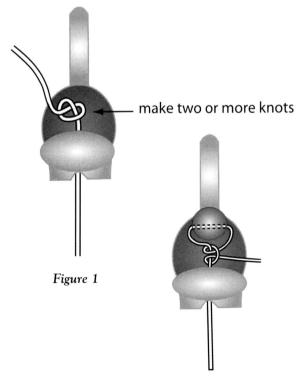

make two or more knots

Figure 1

Figure 2

How to Attach a Clasp Using Cones and Eye Pins

This technique is good for multiple strands. Make your strands and then, if you are using thread, tie the strands together with an overhand knot. Then tie the ends, with one or two double-half hitch knots, to the eye of an eye pin (fig. 1). Secure the knots with glue. Then slip the eye pin into a cone. The cone should cover the knots. Now make a loop in the end of the eye pin that sticks out of the cone. (See fig. 2. To make a loop, see "How to Use a Head Pin or Eye Pin" in this section.) While you are making the loop, attach a clasp to it. When using beading wire or tiger tail, use crimp beads to attach the tiger tail to the eye pin (figs. 3 and 4). You can use cord caps in the same manner as cones.

cut here ←

Figure 1

Figure 2

Figure 3

Figure 4

How to Attach a Clasp Using Cord Tips

To use the crimp-style cord tips to end a piece of jewelry, simply place the cord end onto the middle section of the cord tip (fig. 1). Using chain-nose or flat-nose pliers, fold the cord tip flaps (one side over the other) over the cord and squeeze tight (fig. 2). To use the cup-style cord tip, place a drop of glue inside the tip and then insert the end of the cord into the tip (fig. 3). Let dry. Use a jump ring to attach the loop end of both kinds of tips to a clasp.

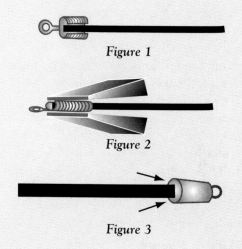

Figure 1

Figure 2

Figure 3

How to Use a Head Pin or Eye Pin

Head pins and eye pins are used mostly to make beaded dangles or earrings. Simply string on beads of your choice and then make a loop on the end of the wire. You can make a plain loop or a wrapped loop. There are two ways to make a plain loop on the end of a head pin or an eye pin. One way is to use flat-nose pliers to make a 90 degree bend in the wire close to the last bead. Cut the wire about 1/4" from the bend. Next, use round-nose pliers to grab the end of the wire and turn the pliers forming the wire into a loop (fig. 1). The other way to make a plain loop on the

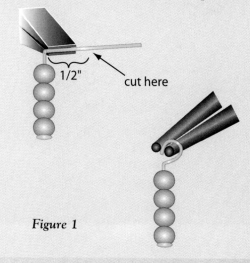

1/2"

cut here

Figure 1

end of a head pin or eye pin is to make a 90 degree bend with flat-nose pliers in the wire close to the last bead. Then grab the wire with round-nose pliers next to the bend and, by hand, wrap the wire around the top jaw of the round-nose pliers (fig. 2). Cut the excess wire and then close the loop with the pliers by squeezing the cut end even with the head pin or eye pin. You can also make a wrapped loop. Wrapped loops are more secure. To make a wrapped loop, you use the flat-nose pliers to make a 90 degree bend in the wire. Grab the wire with the round-nose pliers next to the bend. Then wrap the wire around the jaw of the round nose pliers by hand. Next, using chain-nose pliers or flat-nose pliers (keep holding the loop with the round nose pliers), coil the wire around the head pin or eye pin right under the bend in the wire (fig. 3). You may coil the wire around the eye pin or head pin two, three, or even four times depending on the look you want. When you are done coiling, clip off the excess wire, and then flatten the cut end with pliers.

You can make your own eye pins by making a small loop at one end of a length of wire.

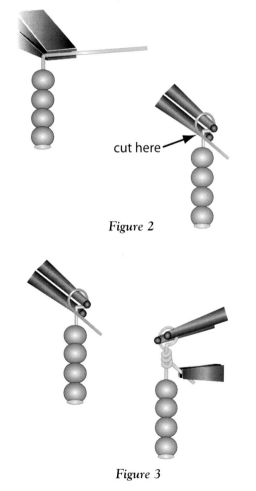

cut here →

Figure 2

Figure 3

How to Make a Jump Ring and How to Open and Close a Jump Ring

To make your own jump rings, get a nail or knitting needle with the desired diameter and wrap your wire around the nail or needle several times. Remove the coil from the nail or needle and, with side-style wire cutters, cut the coil down the center (fig. 1).

To properly open a jump ring, use pliers to spread the ends sideways away from each other (fig. 2). Close a jump ring the same way.

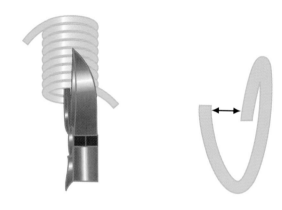

Figure 1   *Figure 2*

How to Tie Knots

The overhand knot is one of the most common knots. It is small, made with one thread (or many threads treated as one). Make a loop in the thread, bring one end of the thread through the loop, and pull tight (fig. 1).

Figure 1

The double-half hitch knot is used with a working thread and a stationary thread. Bring the working thread over and under the stationary thread, then under and over the stationary thread again and through the loop formed by the working thread (fig. 2). Pull tight.

Figure 2

The square knot is a very secure, widely used knot. It is used to tie two threads together. Bring the left-hand thread over and under the right-hand thread, then bring the right-hand thread over and under the left-hand thread (fig. 3). Pull tight.

Figure 3

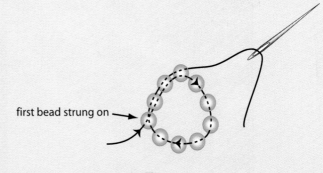

For knotting a bead strand, use overhand knots. To make the overhand knot as close to the beads as possible, put the loop of the knot on the middle of the bead, then hold the thread at the base of the bead with knotting tweezers, and pull the thread end tight with the other hand (fig. 4). It is very important to tie the knots as uniformly as possible and to make all the knots go in the same direction. Do not over-tighten the knots, as this tends to make the strand bunch up or buckle.

Figure 4

How to Tie a Stop Bead

A stop bead is used at the end and/or the beginning of a strand of beads to keep the beads from falling off the thread, and to keep the tension of the beadwork tight. You can make a stop bead by tying a square knot around a bead or you can simply *PNT* the bead twice. This way is not as secure as the square knot, but it is easier to remove (fig. 1).

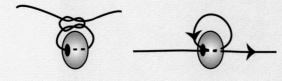

Figure 1

How to Make the Ladder Stitch

Start with a length of thread that has a needle threaded on both ends. String one bead and move it to the center of the thread. * String one bead on one of the needles and then pass the other needle through the bead in the opposite direction. Pull both needles at the same time until the bead is tight up against the first bead * (fig. 1). Repeat between asterisks until the desired length is reached.

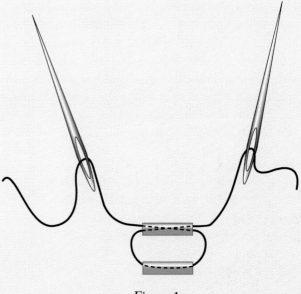

Figure 1

How to Make the Chevron Chain

This stitch is fun and simple. You can easily change the look of the chain by using different beads: bugle beads or bi-cone beads, seed beads or druk beads. Change the color arrangement and the bead count—all these things affect the look you get, but the basic stitch remains the same. To make the chevron chain with seed beads, string on 10 seed beads, *PNBT* the first four beads strung on. This forms the first "stitch" (fig. 1). String on six seed beads then *PNT* the sev-

first bead strung on →

Figure 1

enth bead strung on the first stitch (fig. 2). This is the second "stitch." String six seed beads, *PNT* the fourth bead strung on the second stitch (fig. 3). This is the third "stitch." Repeat the third stitch until the desired length. To use bugle beads for the "Vs" on the chevron chain, string one seed bead, one bugle bead, one seed bead, one bugle bead, and three seed beads. Then *PNBT* the first seed bead, bugle bead, and second seed bead. This forms the first "stitch" (fig. 4). String three seed beads, one bugle bead, and *PNT* the third seed bead strung on the first "stitch." This forms the second "stitch" (fig. 5). String on three seed beads and one bugle bead, *PNT* the third seed bead strung on the second stitch. This is the third "stitch" (fig. 6). Repeat the third "stitch" until the desired length.

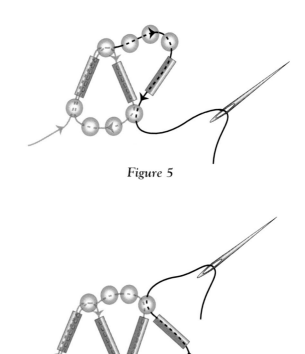

Figure 5

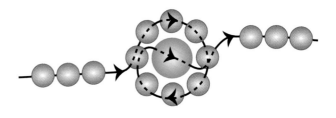

Figure 6

Figure 2

Figure 3

How to Make the Daisy Chain

The two kinds of daisy chain stitches used in this book are the single daisy and the attached daisy.

To make a single daisy chain stitch, string the desired amount of seed beads and then *PNBT* the first bead, forming a circle, the "petal beads." String one bead for the middle of the daisy (usually a different color or size than the "petal beads"). Then *PNT* the bead in the center of the bottom of the "petal beads." This forms the daisy. Several beads are strung on between the daisies (fig. 1).

Figure 4

Figure 1

The attached daisy stitch starts out the same way as the single daisy stitch, but instead of stringing beads between the daisies, you attach the daisies to each other. There are two ways to do this. One way is to string on the desired amount of beads then *PNBT* the first bead forming a circle. Then string on the middle bead and *PNT* a bead on the bottom of the circle. * Next string on two beads, and *PNBT* the two bottom beads of the circle and then *BT* the two just strung on. These are the attachment beads (fig. 2). To make the next daisy, string on the same amount of beads as on the first daisy's circle minus two beads. *PNBT* one of the attachment beads, forming a circle, and then string on the middle bead and *PNT* one of the bottom beads of the circle (fig. 4). * Repeat between asterisks as many times as desired.

The other way to make attached daisies is to string the desired amount of beads and make a circle by *PNBT* the first bead strung on. String on the middle bead, *PNT* a bead from the bottom of the circle then *string on one bead, *PNT* adjacent bead on the circle, string on one bead and then *PNT* the first bead just strung on (fig. 3). String on the same amount of beads from first circle minus two beads. String on the middle bead and *PNT* bead from the bottom of the circle (fig. 4). * Repeat between asterisks as many times as desired.

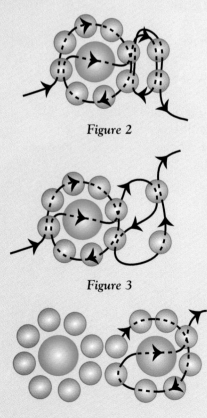

Figure 2

Figure 3

Figure 4

How to Make Vertical Netting

Vertical netting starts out with stringing a base strand. This is simply a strand of the desired beads in the desired length. The rows are vertical and two-sided, the downward side of the row and the upward side. Vertical netting works well with seed beads, but any kind of bead can be used. You can jazz it up with different-sized beads as connecting beads and/or add dangles to the ends. You can also change the number of beads used, so the "holes" of the netting will be smaller or larger. For ease in explaining this stitch, we used blue and green beads. After you make the base strand, *PNBT* some of the base strand beads until the thread is coming out where you want the vertical netting to start.

Row 1
(In this example, we used a one "hole" row.) Downward side of the row—string one green bead, five blue beads, one green, five blues, one green, one blue. *PNBT* one green.

Upward side of the row—string five blues, one green, five blues. *PNT* the first green bead from the downward side of row and then *PNT* the next seven beads on base strand.

Row 2
Downward side of the row—string one green, five blues. *PNT* last green bead from the upward side of the previous row. String five blues, one green, and one blue. *PNBT* one green.

Upward side of the row—string five blues, one green, five blues. *PNT* the first green bead from downward side of the row and then *PNT* the next seven beads on base strand (fig. 1). Repeat Row 2 until the piece has reached the desired length. For longer rows just repeat the downward side of the row for as many numbers of "holes" you want, and do the same for the upward side.

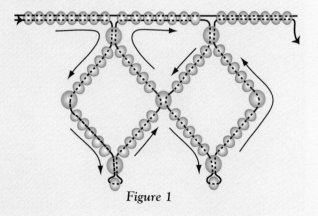

Figure 1

How to Make the Square Stitch

Row 1

String on as many beads as needed for the project.

Row 2 and all others

String two beads, then *PNT* (in the opposite direction of Row 2) second-to-last bead from Row 1 and then back through the second bead just strung on (fig. 1). String one bead, then *PNT* (in the opposite direction of Row 2) the third bead from Row 1, and then back through the bead just strung on. (fig. 2). Continue in this manner stringing on one bead at a time until the end of the row. Remember to make a two-bead stitch at the beginning of each row.

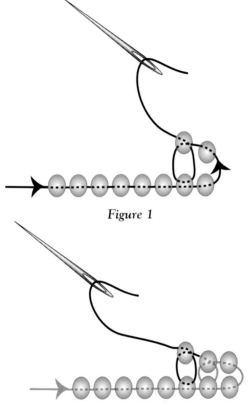

Figure 1

Figure 2

Decrease at the Beginning of the Row

To decrease at the beginning of the row, weave thread back through previous row until the thread comes out of the bead where you want the row to start (fig. 3).

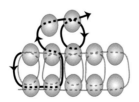

Figure 3

Decrease at the End of the Row

To decrease at the end of the row, simply stop adding beads at the place you want the row to end.

Increase by One Bead

To increase by one bead at the beginning of the row string on two beads, *PNBT* the last bead of previous row, then *PNBT* the second bead just strung on (fig. 4).

To increase by one at the end of the row on two consecutive rows, simply string on one bead and treat it as if it was square-stitched on that row. Then string on two more beads, then *PNBT* the first of the three beads just strung on. *BT* the third bead strung on, and then finish the row in the normal manner (fig. 5).

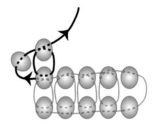

Figure 4

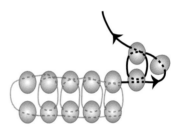

Figure 5

Increase at the Beginning of the Row

To increase at the beginning of the row, string on the desired number of beads, skip the last bead strung on and then *PNBT* the other beads strung on. When you get to the body of the work, start the row as normal (fig. 6).

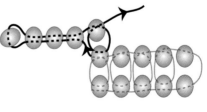

Figure 6

Increase at the End of the Row

To increase at the end of the row simply string on the amount of beads that you want to increase by and, on the next row, treat them as if they had been square stitched (fig. 7).

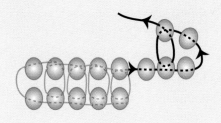

Figure 7

How to Make the Right Angle Weave Stitch

Row 1

String on four beads. *PNBT* the first three beads strung on. This forms the first stitch. * String on three beads and *PNT* the end bead of the first stitch and back through the first two beads strung on. This forms the second stitch (fig. 1). * Repeat between asterisks for the desired number of stitches. In each stitch the thread alternates directions.

Row 2

If you ended Row 1 with the thread coming out of the top of the end bead, then *PNBT* the top bead of last stitch from Row 1. String on three beads. *PNBT* top bead from Row 1 and then *PNBT* the first of the three beads strung on. This is the first stitch of Row 2. String on three beads. Then *PNT* (in the opposite direction from Row 2) the top bead of the next stitch from Row 1. Then *PNBT* the end bead of the previous stitch and both beads just strung on. This is the second stitch of Row 2. Then *PNT* the top bead of the stitch from Row 1 (fig. 2). String on two beads. *PNT* end bead of previous stitch, and the next top bead from Row 1 and through the first bead strung on. This is the third stitch of Row 2. Continue in this manner adding two beads for each stitch until desired length. As in Row 1, the thread will alternate directions in each stitch.

If you ended the Row 1 with the thread coming out of the bottom of the end bead, then for the second row you must *PNT* the other three beads of this last stitch. The thread is now coming out of the top bead from the last stitch with the needle facing in the same direction as the first row.

Now string on three beads and *PNBT* the top bead then *BT* the three beads just strung on. This is the first stitch. Next *PNT* the top bead from the next stitch on previous row (fig. 3). String on two beads then *PNBT* the end bead from the stitch you just made and *BT* the top bead and the first bead you just strung on. This forms the second stitch. Now string on two beads, *PNT* the top bead from the next stitch from Row 1 (going in the opposite direction of Row 2). Then *PNT* the end bead from the previous stitch and *BT* the two beads just strung on. This is the third stitch. Repeat the second and third stitches until the desired length. The rest of the rows are a repeat of Row 2.

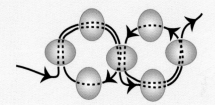

Figure 1

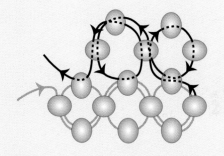

Figure 2

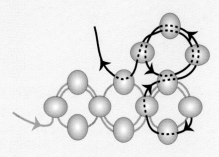

Figure 3

How to Make Even-Count Peyote Stitch and Even-Count Tubular Peyote Stitch

The flat peyote stitch used in this book is the even-count flat peyote. To make even-count flat peyote, you must first string on an even number of beads.

These beads will make up the first two rows. For Row 3, string one bead then skip a bead and *PNT* the next bead (fig. 1). String a bead, skip a bead and *PNT* the next bead (fig. 2). Repeat until the end of the beads. For Row 4: On this row it will be easy to identify which beads are on each row. The beads from the last row will definitely be higher than the beads from the previous row. *String one bead *PNT* next stepped up bead.* Repeat between asterisks until the end of the row. Continue in this manner until the desired length.

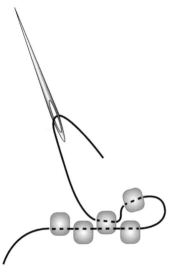

Figure 1

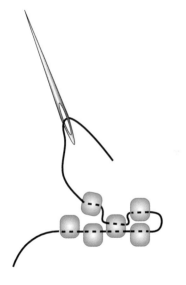

Figure 2

To do even-count tubular peyote stitch, string on an even number of beads. *PNBT* the first bead strung on forming a circle. These beads will form rounds one

and two. Keep the circle tight by holding the tail of thread. You will have an odd number of beads for each round. (This is called Even-Count Tubular Peyote because you start with an even number of beads, but the beads-per-round end up being an odd number.)

Round 3: String one bead, skip a bead, from the bead circle, *PNT* the next bead from the bead circle (fig. 3). * String one bead, skip a bead, *PNT* next bead (fig. 4). * Repeat between asterisks until the end of the circle. *PNBT* first bead from this round, so that the needle is properly positioned for the next round. Pull tight.

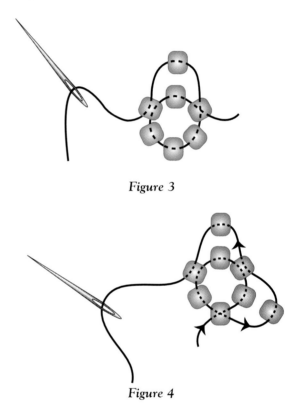

Figure 3

Figure 4

Round 4: On this round it will be easy to identify which beads are on each round. The beads will be definitely higher from Round 3 than the beads from Round 2. * String one bead, *PNT* the next stepped up bead. * Repeat between asterisks until the end of the round. Then *PNBT* the first bead of the round so that the needle is positioned properly for the next round. Pull tight. Continue in this manner until the piece is the desired length.

3

Bead Stranding Projects

The very first beading technique was the bead strand. Small fossil sponges with natural holes in them were found in England lying together in graduated sizes—suggesting they were made into a necklace some 50,000 years ago. Bead strands are the most basic of beaded adornment. In this chapter, we have included seven strand projects, one twisted-strand project, and two braided-strand projects.

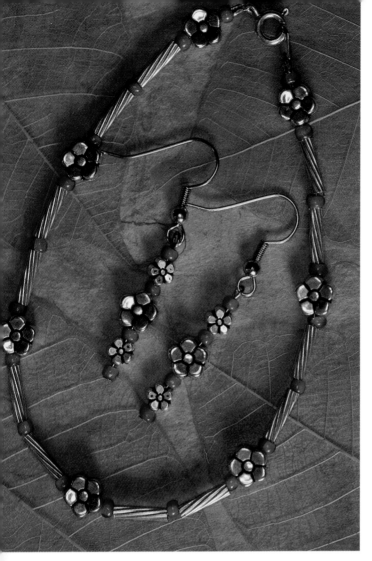

Metal Flower Anklet and Earrings

ANKLET

MATERIALS

14 twisted silver metal bugle beads 3/8" long
20 pink white-heart (or color you prefer) seed beads, size 8°
5 silver metal flower beads, 7mm (or whatever kind of metal bead that suites your fancy)
2 silver crimp beads, size 2mm (or size to fit your beading wire)
1 silver spring ring clasp
Beading wire size .018", 1-1/2 yards

TOOLS

Wire cutters
Crimp pliers

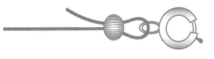

Figure 1

Figure 2

Figure 3

Step 1
Attaching One End of the Clasp

Using about 1 yard of beading wire, string one crimp bead, then one end of the clasp. Bring the wire back through the crimp bead. Pull tight (fig. 1). Squeeze crimp bead with crimp pliers. Cut off excess wire to about 1/2".

Step 2
Stringing the Beads

String on beads in this order (make sure the first few beads go over both strands of wire. See fig. 2):
* one pink, one flower, one pink, one bugle, one pink, one bugle. * Repeat between asterisks five times then string on one pink, one flower, one pink.

Step 3
Attaching the Other End of the Clasp

String on a crimp bead then a jump ring or tab whichever you are using for your clasp, then thread wire back through the crimp bead and pull tight making sure beads are tight up against crimp bead and tab. Squeeze crimp bead with crimp pliers. Cut excess wire to 1/2" and pass back through the beads to hide (fig. 3).

EARRINGS

MATERIALS

2 silver metal flower beads, 7mm
4 silver metal flower beads, 5mm
8 pink white-heart seed beads, size 8°
2 silver head pins
1 pair silver fishhook ear wires

TOOLS

Flat-nose pliers
Crimp pliers

Step 1
Stringing the Beads onto a Head Pin

String beads onto head pin in this order: one pink, one small flower, one pink, one large flower, one pink, one small flower, one pink.

Step 2
Attaching the Earring Wires

Using flat-nose pliers, make a 90-degree bend in the wire close to the last bead (fig. 4). With round-nose pliers, grab the wire as close to the bend as possible and, with your free hand, turn the wire around the jaw of the pliers into a loop (fig. 5). Slip the earring wire onto the loop, cut the excess wire, and close the loop (fig. 6). Repeat Steps 1 and 2 for second earring.

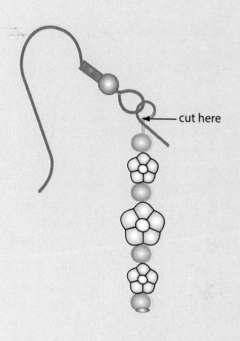

Figure 6

Figure 4

Figure 5

Using the same technique as the anklet, you can create different styles of jewelry by changing the beads, colors, and arrangements.

Lemon Necklace and Bracelet

Step 1
Attaching One End of the Clasp
Using about 1-1/2 yards of beading wire, string a crimp bead, then one end of the clasp. Bring the wire back through the crimp bead. Pull tight. Squeeze the crimp bead with the crimp pliers. Cut the excess wire to about 1" (fig. 1).

Figure 1

Step 2
Stringing the Beads
String *one druk, one yellow transparent, one purple triangle, one yellow transparent, one druk, one yellow transparent, one purple triangle, one yellow transparent, one druk, one yellow transparent, one purple triangle, one yellow transparent. String on one druk, and one lemon bead.* Make sure the first few beads go over both strands of wire to hide the excess. Repeat between the asterisks three times. Next string on one druk, one lemon, one druk and one lemon. For the other half of the necklace repeat between the asterisks three times then string on one druk, one transparent yellow, one triangle, one transparent yellow, one druk, one transparent yellow, one triangle, one transparent yellow, one druk, one transparent yellow, one triangle, one transparent yellow, one druk.

NECKLACE

MATERIALS

24 purple silver-lined triangle beads, size 6°
48 transparent yellow seed beads, size 8°
34 yellow druk beads, 4mm
9 glass lemon beads
2 gold crimp beads
1 gold hook and eye clasp
Beading wire, size .012, 1-1/2 yards

TOOLS

Crimp pliers

Step 3
Attaching the Other End of the Clasp

String on a crimp bead then the other end of the clasp. Thread the wire back through the crimp bead and pull tight, making sure beads are tight up against the crimp bead and the clasp. Squeeze the crimp bead with the crimp pliers. Cut the excess wire to about 1" and hide the end by passing the wire back through the beads.

BRACELET

MATERIALS

8 purple silver-lined triangle beads, size 6°
16 transparent yellow seed beads, size 8°
16 yellow druk beads, 4mm
7 yellow glass lemon beads
2 gold crimp beads
1 gold hook and eye clasp
Beading wire, size .012, 1 yard

TOOLS

Crimp pliers

Step 1
Attaching One End of the Clasp

Using 1 yard of beading wire, repeat Step 1 from the necklace instructions.

Step 2
Stringing the Beads

String *one druk, one transparent yellow, one triangle, one transparent yellow, one druk, one lemon bead.* Make sure the first few beads go over both strands of wire to hide the excess. Repeat between the asterisks six times. Then string on one druk, one transparent yellow, one triangle, one transparent yellow and one druk.

Step 3
Attaching the Other End of the Clasp

Repeat Step 3 from the necklace instructions.

Black and Silver Necklace and Earrings

Step 1
Attaching the Clasp

Cut a length of tiger tail 20" long. String on one crimp bead, and one end of the clasp. Then pass the tiger tail back through the crimp bead. This will form a loop with the clasp on it. Pull tiger tail end tight so the crimp bead is close to the clasp. Leave a short 1" tail (fig. 1). Squeeze the crimp bead with the crimp pliers.

Figure 1

NECKLACE

MATERIALS

10 small silver flat flower or spacer beads
4 metal accent beads
26 gray transparent silver-lined seed beads, size 10°
18 silver lined twist bugle beads, 15mm
4 black oval faceted beads, 7mm x 5mm
1 round faceted smoky gray crystal bead, 12mm
2 silver bead caps
2 crimp beads
Beading wire or tiger tail, size .018, 1 yard
1 torpedo clasp (skinny barrel clasp), 10mm

TOOLS

Crimp pliers
Wire cutters

Step 2
Stringing the Beads

String on one gray seed bead, * one bugle bead, and one gray seed bead. * Repeat between the asterisks five times. String on one metal accent bead, one gray seed bead, one bugle, one gray seed bead, one small spacer, one black oval faceted, one small spacer, one gray seed bead, one bugle, one gray seed bead, one small spacer, one black oval faceted, one small spacer, one gray seed bead, one bugle, one gray seed bead, one small spacer, one metal accent, one silver bead cap, one gray crystal (12mm), one silver bead cap, one metal accent, one small spacer, one gray seed bead, one bugle, one gray seed bead, one small spacer, one black oval faceted, one small spacer, one gray seed bead, one bugle, one gray seed bead, one small spacer, one black oval faceted, one small spacer, one gray seed bead, one bugle, one gray seed bead, one metal accent, one gray seed bead, * one bugle, one gray seed bead. * Repeat between the asterisks five times.

Step 3
Attaching the Clasp
Attach this clasp end the same way as you did the other end. Leave a 1" tail and pass it through the beads until the tail is hidden in beads.

EARRINGS

MATERIALS

2 metal accent beads
8 gray transparent silver-lined seed beads, size 10°
2 silver-lined twist bugle beads, 15mm
2 round faceted smoky gray crystal bead, 12mm
2 silver bead caps
2 silver head pins
2 silver fishhook ear wires

TOOLS

Flat-nose pliers
Round-nose pliers

Step 1
Making the Dangles
On a head pin, place one gray seed bead, one bead cap, one smoky gray crystal, one bead cap, one gray seed bead, one bugle, one gray seed bead, one metal accent, one gray seed bead.

Step 2
Attaching the Earring Wires
With flat-nose pliers, bend the head pin close to the beads in a 90-degree angle. Slip on an earring wire, then with a round-nose pliers make a loop, and cut off the excess wire. Repeat Steps 1 and 2 for the other earring.

Tooth Necklace and Earrings

NECKLACE

MATERIALS

3, 5 or 7 baby teeth (or gemstone chips to match the jasper)

1 strand of 4mm fossil beads natural color, 16" length (or 4mm fancy jasper)

1 gold barrel clasp or your favorite clasp

3, 5 or 7 bell caps, large and/or medium and/or small to fit teeth or gemstone chips

2 gold crimp beads

Beading wire, size .012, 1 yard

TOOLS

Crimp pliers
Bonding glue

Step 1
Attaching the Teeth (Gemstone Chips) to the Bell Caps

Insert one end of a tooth or chip into the bell cap and use the flat-nosed pliers to carefully adjust the legs of the bell cap to fit the shape of the tooth or chip. Depending on the size of the teeth or chips you have chosen, you will use either large, medium, or small bell caps. We used both small and medium bell caps on this necklace. Now remove the tooth or chip from the bell cap and drop a dab of bonding glue into the bell cap. Reinsert the tooth or chip, giving the bell cap legs a final adjustment (fig. 1). Set aside until glue dries. Repeat as many times as you have objects. Odd numbers seem to work the best. We used seven and three in these examples.

Figure 1

Have you ever wondered what to do with those baby teeth that the "tooth fairy" removes from under the pillow? Well, you need not wonder any longer. Make a keepsake necklace and matching earrings! If you have no children, puppies' or kittens' baby teeth will do just fine. And for those who find the thought of a tooth necklace offensive, you can use stone chips.

Step 2
Stringing the Beads

Using about one yard of beading wire, string one crimp bead then one end of the clasp. Bring the wire back through the crimp bead. Pull tight. Squeeze the crimp bead with crimp pliers. Cut off the excess wire to about 1/2". String on 36 fossil beads (or fancy jasper), making sure the first few beads go over both strands of wire. Then string on one molar-type tooth, four fossil beads, one incisor-type tooth, four fossil beads, one incisor-type tooth, four fossil beads, one puppy tooth. Now repeat backwards after the puppy tooth so that it is symmetrical. Then string on 36 fossil beads. Replace the teeth with gemstone chips if you prefer. Adjust the bead count and spacing, if you have fewer teeth to use. We didn't use jump rings on the bell caps of the teeth, but we did on the green gemstone necklace; it depends on the look you want. If you do want to use jump rings, attach a jump ring to each bell cap and string the beading wire through the jump ring.

Step 3
Attaching the Other End of the Clasp

String on a crimp bead then the other end of the clasp. Bring the wire back through the crimp bead and pull tight. Make sure beads are tight against the crimp bead and clasp. Squeeze the crimp bead with crimp pliers. Cut the excess wire to 1/2" and pass it back through the beads to hide.

Tooth Earrings

MATERIALS
2 baby teeth (or gemstone chips)
2 bell caps
2 fishhook ear wires
2 jump rings

TOOLS
Crimping pliers
Bonding glue

Step 1
Attaching the Bell Caps

Attach a bell cap to each tooth or chip using the same instructions as the tooth necklace.

Step 2
Attaching the Ear Wire

Use a jump ring to attach the bell cap to the earring wire (fig. 2). Repeat Steps 1 and 2 for the other earring.

Figure 2

Using stones instead of teeth.

Pink Stretchy Bracelets and Earrings

BRACELET

MATERIALS

23 lantern-cut Swarovski crystals, 4mm
1 small tube of light pink seed beads, size 11°
White stretchy floss (fibrous elastic) or
.5mm clear stretchy cord, 3 yards

TOOLS

Twisted wire bead needle
Bonding glue

Step 1
Stringing the Beads

Using about 1 yard of floss and the twisted beading needle, string 31 light pink beads, then one crystal. Repeat three times. Strand should measure 7". Make one more. Then for the third bracelet, string beads in the following pattern: 10 light pink, one crystal, three pink, one crystal, three pink, one crystal. Repeat four times.

Step 2
Tying Off the Stretchy Floss

When you are done stringing the beads, tie a square knot (right over left, then left over right) keeping the beads tightly together. Thread the tails into the beads on either side of the knot (fig. 1). Place a dab of glue on the knot and wiggle it so the glue also goes into the holes of the beads on either side to hold the tails in the beads. Let dry, then cut off excess floss. Repeat for each bracelet.

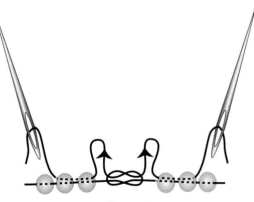

Figure 1

EARRINGS

MATERIALS

8 lantern cut Swarovski crystals, 4mm
62 light pink seed beads, size 11°
White beading thread, 2 yards
2 bead tips
2 lever back ear wires

TOOLS

Beading needle, size 12
Flat-nose pliers
Round-nose pliers
Bonding glue

Step 1
Stringing the Beads and Attaching a Bead Tip

Thread a beading needle with about 1 yard of beading thread. String on one clamshell bead tip, one crystal, 12 pink seed beads, one crystal, three pink, one crystal, three pink, one crystal, 12 pink. *PNBT* the first crystal and bead tip forming a loop (fig. 2). String on one pink seed bead and tie a

square knot using both thread ends (fig. 3). Place a drop of glue on the knot and squeeze the bead tip closed (using flat-nose pliers) over the knot and the seed bead.

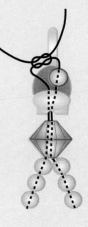

Figure 3

Step 2
Attaching the Ear Wire

Slip earring wire onto bead tip and using round-nose pliers turn bead tip hook closed around earring wire loop. Repeat Steps 1 and 2 for second earring.

Figure 2

Grapes Necklace and Earrings

NECKLACE

MATERIALS

10 transparent green leaf beads, 7mm x 12mm
10 gms purple iris seed beads, size 11°
16 transparent lavender silver-lined triangle
    beads, size 5°
14 transparent green-lined topaz triangle beads,
    size 5°
4 transparent green cube beads, 5mm
1 transparent green round bead, 7mm
5 grape beads (or other novelty beads if you can't
    find grapes with the hole at the top)
1 gold lobster claw clasp
Nymo beading thread, black, size B, 4-1/2 yards
2 gold eye pins

TOOLS

Beading needle, size 11
Round-nose pliers
Flat-nose pliers
Wire cutters

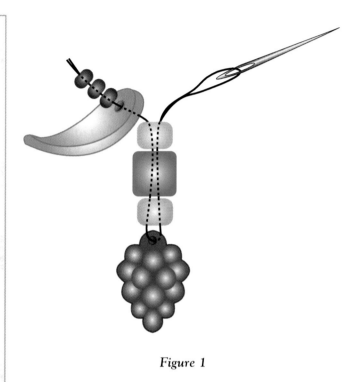

Figure 1

Step 1
Stringing the Beads

Using about 2 yards of doubled thread, tie a stop bead at the end of the thread leaving a 6" tail. String on 2-1/4" of purple iris seed beads, then * one green lined topaz triangle bead, one lavender triangle and one green lined triangle. Then string 7/8" of the purple iris seed beads. * Repeat between the asterisks two times.

Step 2
Making the Grape Dangle

* String on one leaf bead, one lavender triangle, one green cube bead, one lavender triangle, one grape bead, then *PNBT* one lavender triangle, one green cube bead, one lavender triangle (fig. 1). String on one leaf, and 10 purple iris seed beads. * Repeat between the asterisks one more time. Make the middle dangle the same as the other two, except instead of the green cube bead, string on the 7mm green round bead, and when done with the dangle, string on the 10 purple iris seed beads. Then repeat between the asterisks two more times. On the last repeat, instead of 10 purple iris beads, string on 7/8" of the purple iris beads. Repeat between the asterisks from Step 1 three times, but on the last repeat, instead of 7/8" of purple iris beads, string on 2-1/4" of purple iris beads. Set aside.

Step 3
Making the Eye Pin Clasp Ends of the Necklace

Put one green lined triangle bead onto an eye pin. Pass the long end of the eye pin wire into the clasp loop and make an eyelet on the end (fig. 2). Repeat for the other end of the clasp.

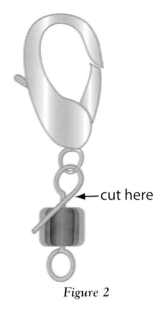

←—cut here

Figure 2

Step 4
Attaching the Clasp Ends to the Necklace

Now, using the end of thread on the necklace, *PNT* one of the eyelets several times, pull tight and tie two knots. *PNBT* about 1/2" of the purple iris beads to hide the thread and cut off the excess (fig. 3). Remove stop bead from the other end of the necklace and repeat Step 4 using the other beaded eyelet.

Figure 3

EARRINGS

MATERIALS

18 purple iris seed beads, size 11°
4 transparent green lined topaz triangle beads, size 5°
2 transparent lavender triangle beads, size 5°
4 transparent green leaf beads
2 grape beads
2 gold fishhook ear wires
Nymo beading thread, size B, 2 yards

TOOLS

Beading needle, size 11

Step 1
Making the Grape Earrings

Use about 1 yard of doubled thread. String on a grape bead leaving about a 12" tail. String on one lavender triangle, one leaf bead, one green lined triangle, nine purple iris seed beads. *PNT* the loop of one of the earring wires (fig. 4). String on one lined green triangle bead, one leaf bead, then *PNBT* the lavender triangle, grape bead and *BT* the lavender triangle. Now *PNBT* all the beads, and then tie a square knot with the tail thread and the needle thread (fig. 5). Pass both the thread ends through several of the beads to hide and then cut off the excess. Repeat for second earring.

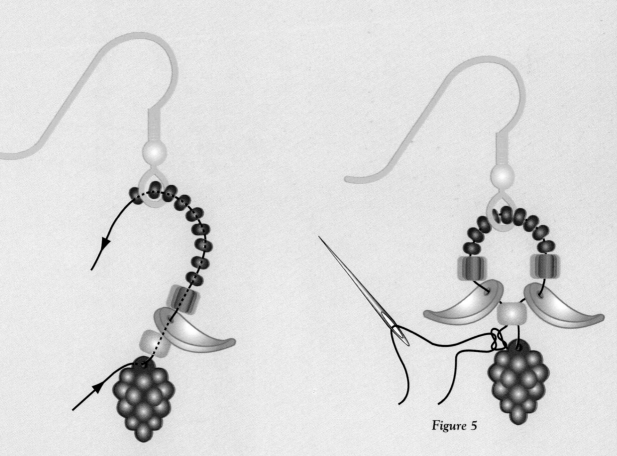

Figure 4

Figure 5

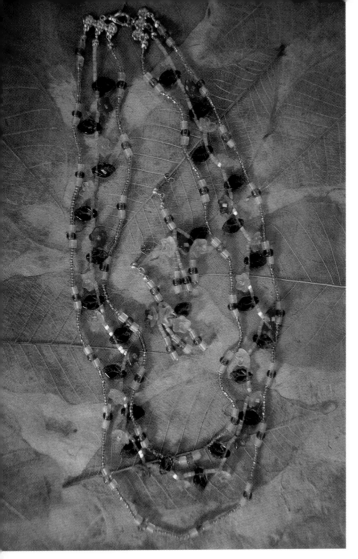

Three-Strand Flower Necklace and Earrings

NECKLACE

MATERIALS

23 transparent green leaf beads
8 dark pink flower beads with the hole in the middle
7 light amber flower beads
7 light pink flower beads
10 gms bronze silver-lined seed beads, size 11°
34 transparent amber seed beads, size 8°
68 matte light amber square beads, 3.5mm x 4mm
196 light yellow satin beads
1 gold lobster claw clasp
2 jump rings
2 three-strand separators
6 gold bead tips
Nymo beading thread, tan, size F, 12 yards

TOOLS

Round-nose pliers
Flat-nose pliers
Scissors
Beading needle, size 11

Step 1
Making the Strands

Strand 1

Thread a needle with doubled thread 2 yards long. Attach a bead tip to the end of the thread. (See Techniques, page 22.) * String on one square bead, one size 8° amber bead, one square bead, 15 bronze size 11° seed beads. * Repeat between asterisks 17 times then string on one square bead, one size 8° amber bead, one square bead. Attach bead tip to the end and set aside. The strand should measure 22-1/2" (excluding the bead tips).

Strand 2

Thread needle with doubled thread 2 yards long. Attach a bead tip to the end of the thread. String on 10 satin beads, one leaf bead, * four satin beads, one dark pink flower bead, one satin bead, and then *PNBT* the flower bead. (See fig. 1. When stringing on the flower bead, *PNT* the backside of the flower first and then *BT* the front of the bead.)

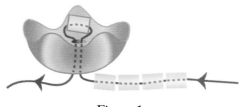

Figure 1

String on four satin beads, one leaf bead, four satin beads, one light pink flower bead, one satin bead, *PNBT* flower bead. String on four satin beads, one leaf bead, four satin beads, one light amber flower bead, one satin bead, *PNBT* flower bead. String on four satin beads, one leaf bead. * Repeat between asterisks six times then string on four satin beads, one dark pink flower bead, one satin bead, *PNBT* flower bead. String on four satin beads, one leaf bead, 10 satin beads. Attach a bead tip as close to the beads as possible. Strand should measure 20-1/4" excluding bead tips. When stringing this strand make sure you push the flower beads close to their neighboring beads, so that you won't get unsightly gaps in the bead strand.

Strand 3
Thread a needle with about 2 yards of doubled thread. Attach a bead tip at the end of the thread. String 10 bronze size 11° seed beads, * one square bead, one amber size 8° bead, one square bead, 15 bronze size 11° beads. * Repeat between the asterisks 13 times then string on one square bead, one amber size 8° bead, one square bead, and 10 bronze size 11° seed beads. Attach a bead tip as close to the beads as possible. The strand should measure 18-1/2" excluding the bead tip.

Step 4
Attaching the Strands to Separators and Clasps
Hold the two separators with the one-loop-edge on top and the three-loop-edge on the bottom, then you will attach Strand #1 to the right most loop on the right-hand-side separator and the left most loop on the left-hand-side separator, so Strand #1 becomes the bottom most strand. Attach Strand #2 to the middle loops and it becomes the middle strand. Attach Strand #3 to the remaining loops and it becomes the top strand. Now attach the clasp ends to the separators.

EARRINGS

MATERIALS
2 transparent green leaf beads
2 dark pink flower beads with the hole in the middle
2 light amber flower beads
2 light pink flower beads
6 bronze silver lined seed beads, size 11°
8 transparent amber seed beads, size 8°
16 matte light amber square beads, 3.5mm x 4mm
56 light yellow satin beads
1 pair gold drop ear studs
2 gold bead tips
Nymo beading thread, tan, size F, 2 yards

TOOLS
Round-nose pliers
Flat-nose pliers
Scissors
Beading needle, size 11

Step 1
Stringing the Beads
Thread needle with about 1 yard of thread and string on one square bead, one amber size 8° bead, one square bead, four satins. String on one dark pink flower bead, one satin bead and *PNBT* flower bead. (See fig. 1 from the necklace.) String on six satins, one square, one amber size 8°, one square, and one bronze seed bead. *PNBT* one square, one size 8°, one square, six satins, four satins (fig. 2). For next dangle, string on four satin, one leaf, one light amber flower, one satin, *PNBT* the flower bead. String on four satins, four squares, one size 8°, one square, one bronze. *PNBT* one square, one size 8°, one square, four satins, one leaf, four satins. For third dangle, string on four satins, one light pink flower, one satin, *PNBT* flower bead. String on six satins, one square, one size 8°, one square, one bronze. *PNBT* one square, one size 8°, one square, six satins, four satins and then *PNBT* the first square, one size 8° and one square bead strung on. String on bead tip with both thread ends and attach bead tip to thread and then attach drop ear stud to bead tip. Make two.

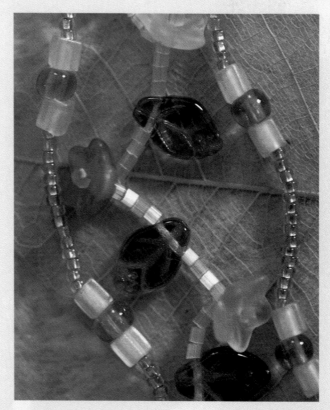

Figure 2

Seven-Strand Twist Necklace and Eyeglass Chain

NECKLACE

MATERIALS

2 large-holed turquoise beads, 10mm
1 hank of crystal gold-lined seed beads, size 10°
187 matte silver-lined transparent teal size seed beads, 6°
1/2 hank of opaque aqua seed beads, size 11°
2 silver eye pins
2 silver cones
2 silver jump rings
1 silver magnetic clasp
Nymo beading thread, black or blue, size F, 14 yards

TOOLS

Round-nose pliers
Flat-nose pliers
Beading needle, size 11
Bonding glue

Step 1
Stringing the Beads
Use 1-yard lengths of doubled thread. Make four crystal gold lined bead strands, 17" long, one matte teal size 6° bead strand, 17" long, and two aqua size 11° bead strands, 17" long. Place a stop bead at each end of the strands and leave about a 10" tail at the ends.

Step 2
Attaching the Cone and the Clasp End
Gather all the strands together and carefully remove the stop beads on one end of the strands. Tie all the strands together in a single overhand knot. Make the knot as close to the beads as possible. Slip a large-holed turquoise bead over all the strand ends and the overhand knot. Next, tie the strand ends to the eyelet of an eye pin using several knots. Place a dab of glue over the knots and clip the excess thread ends. Place one cone over the eye pin and make an eyelet on the end of the eye pin with the pliers. (See Techniques, page 22 for detailed instructions.) Attach a jump ring to the eyelet and one end of the clasp to the jump ring.

Step 3
Twisting the Strands

Gather the four strands of the crystal gold lined beads and twist together. Then take the remaining three strands and twist them around the crystal gold lined strands. Try to keep the aqua strands on opposite sides of the teal bead strand when twisting (fig. 1).

Step 4
Attaching the Other Cone and Clasp End

Carefully untie the stop beads from the ends of the strands, adjust the twists, if necessary, and make an overhand knot with all the strands. Make the knot as close to the beads as possible. Slip thread ends through a large-holed turquoise bead and cover the knot with it. Tie strands to an eyelet and attach a cone and the other end of the clasp as done in Step 2.

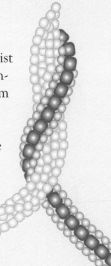

Figure 1

Eye Glass Chain

MATERIALS

378 crystal gold-lined seed beads, size 10°
28 matte silver-lined transparent teal seed beads, size 6°
168 opaque aqua seed beads, size 11°
2 silver bead tips, clamshell style
2 silver jump rings
Nymo beading thread, black or blue, size F, 6 yards

TOOLS

Round-nose pliers
Flat-nose pliers
Bonding glue
Beading needle, size 11

Step 1
Attaching the Bead Tip and Stringing the Beads onto Two Threads

Thread two needles each with doubled thread, about 1-1/2 yards long. String a bead tip onto both needles and slip the bead tip down to the end of the threads

and tie two square knots in the bead tip. Cut off excess thread and place a drop of glue on the knots. Squeeze the bead tip closed over the knots with the flat-nose pliers. * Next, using both needles, string on three aqua beads, one teal bead, three aqua (fig. 2). String seven crystal gold-lined beads onto one needle, then do the same for the other needle (fig. 3). * Repeat between asterisks 26 more times, and to finish it off string three aqua, one teal, three aqua. Piece should measure 25".

Figure 2

Figure 3

Step 2
Attaching the Other Bead Tip and Eyeglass Chain Findings

Attach a bead tip the same way as in Step 1, making sure you keep the bead tip close to the end beads. Slip the eyeglass chain finding onto the hook of the bead tip and turn the hook closed with the round-nose pliers. Do the same for the other end.

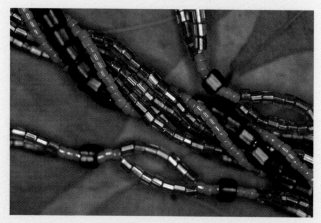

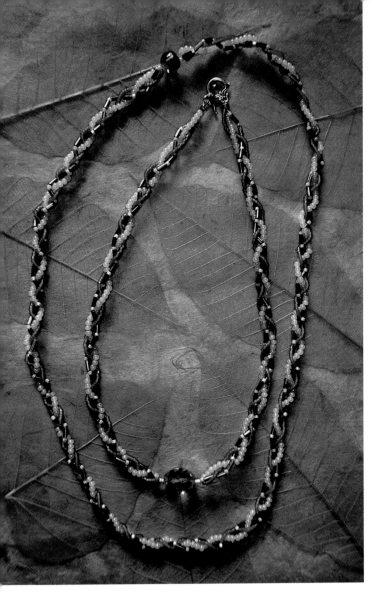

Three-Strand Braided Necklace and Headband

NECKLACE

MATERIALS

Light blue matte Japanese tubular beads
White iridescent seed beads, size 8°
Green iris bugle beads, 4mm
White Japanese tubular beads
1 oval faceted glass light blue and green bead,
    14mm x 10mm
2 crimp beads, 4mm
1 toggle clasp
Beading wire, size .018, 4 yards

TOOLS

Crimp pliers
Bonding glue
Masking tape

Step 1
Attaching One End of the Clasp

Cut three strands of beading wire, each 4 feet long. Slip a crimp bead on all three strands, then slip one end of the clasp onto all three strands. Pass all three strands back through crimp bead, forming a small loop. Squeeze crimp bead with crimp pliers.

Step 2
Stringing the Beads

String one of the strands with white size 8° beads, one with light blue tubular beads and the third one following this pattern: One white tubular, one green bugle, one white, one bugle. Make each strand about 10-1/2" long. Tie a stop bead on each end. Don't worry about the beading wire getting a few bends in it since this part of the wire will be hidden in the large faceted bead.

Step 3
Braiding the Strands

Attach the end with the clasp to a table or a flat surface using masking tape. Separate the strands and lay them flat. Braid them together: Take the strand on the right and bring it over the middle strand (fig. 1). Next, take the strand on the left and bring it over the newly-created middle strand (fig. 2). Repeat until the braid measures 7-1/2". When you get to the end you might have to remove some beads on one or two of the strands to even them up. All three should be the same length. Carefully remove stop beads, then hold the braid end tight in one hand, and string two white tubular beads onto all three strands. Push the white beads tight up against the braid, then string on the faceted glass bead and two more white tubular beads onto all strands.

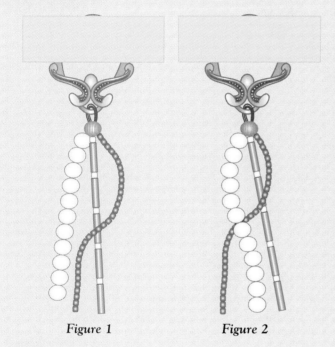

Figure 1   Figure 2

Step 4
Stringing the Beads on the Other Half of the Necklace

Remove the necklace from the table and string one of the strands with white size 8° seed beads, one with light blue tubular beads and one with this pattern: one green bugle, one white tubular, one bugle, one white. All strands should measure about 10-1/2". Tie a stop bead to each end.

Step 5
Braiding the Strands and Attaching the Other End of the Clasp

Braid the three strands together the same way you did in Step 3. When the braid measures 7-1/2" stop braid-

ing, remove any excess beads and the stop beads. String a crimp bead onto all three strands, then string on the other end of the clasp. Pass the three strands back through the crimp bead and pull tight so that the crimp bead is close to the braid, and the clasp loop is close to the crimp bead. Squeeze the crimp bead with crimp pliers and pass excess beading wire back through several beads then cut off the excess wire.

HEADBAND

MATERIALS

Light blue matte Japanese tubular beads
White iridescent seed beads, size 8°
Green iris bugle beads, 4mm
White Japanese tubular beads
1 large-holed green pony bead
1mm stretchy bead cord, 4 yards

TOOLS

Bonding glue
Masking tape

Step 1
Stringing the Beads

Cut three lengths of stretchy cord, about 4 feet each. Tie a stop bead on the ends of each strand. String one of the strands with light blue tubular beads, one strand with white size 8° beads, and on the other one follow the pattern: one bugle bead, one white tubular bead, one bugle, one white. The strands should measure 32". Push beads tight together and then tie a stop bead at each end.

Step 2
Braiding the Strands

Remove the stop beads from one side of the strands, then tie the three strands together using an overhand knot (fig. 3). Attach the ends that are tied together to a table or some other flat surface using masking tape. Separate the strands and lay them flat. Braid them together: Take the strand on the right and bring it over the middle strand (see fig. 1 from the necklace instructions). Next, take the strand on the left and bring it over the newly-

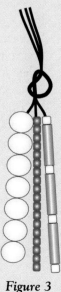

Figure 3

created middle strand (see fig. 2 from the necklace instructions). Repeat until braid measures about 21" or size to fit around your head. When you get to the end of the braid you may have to remove some beads on one or two of the strands to even them up. All three should be the same length. Carefully remove stop beads then tie the strands together using an overhand knot. Remove strands from the table.

Step 3
Tying the Ends Together

String the large green pony bead on one end of the braid and push it over the overhand knot then tie the two ends of the braid together using a square knot. Pull tight and cut off excess stretchy cord. Cover the knots with glue and slip the pony bead over the knots to hide them while the glue is still wet. Let dry.

Seven-Strand Braided Bracelet and Barrette

BRACELET

MATERIALS

Gold lined seed beads, size 11°
Pink white heart seed beads, size 8°
Blue iris twist bugle beads, 1/4" long
Gold AB luster bugle beads, 1/4" long
Pink matte twist bugle beads, 1/4" long
Bronze triangle beads
Matte iris AB triangle beads
2 gold cones
2 gold clamshells
1 gold lobster claw clasp
2 gold jump rings
Nymo beading thread, black, size B, 7 yards

TOOLS

Beading needle, size 12, or whatever size fits your
    beads
Bonding glue
Masking tape

Step 1
Stranding the Beads

Thread the beading needle onto a one-yard length of
thread. Tie on a stop bead leaving at least a 6" tail.
Then string gold beads until strand measures 9". Set
aside. Repeat with all the other colors, so you have a
9" strand of each color. Pick up all seven strands and
tie them together in an overhand knot using the end
of the strands without the stop bead. Tie the knot as
close to the beads as possible.

Step 2
Braiding the Strands

Attach the knot to a table or other flat surface using masking tape. Lay all the strands flat. * Pick up the right-most strand and bring it over three strands then lay it down (fig. 1). Next, bring the left-most strand over three strands and lay it down (fig. 2). If you feel comfortable, you may hold all the strands in your hands while braiding. Keep the tension fairly tight. * Repeat between asterisks until you come to the end of the beads. The braid should measure 6". This measurement will vary depending on how tightly or loosely you braid. You might have to braid it over again if it is way too long or too short. Remove the stop beads making sure you hold the braid tight so it won't unravel. At this time also remove any excess beads, as the braiding process will make some of the strands longer than the others. Tie the strands into an overhand knot the same way you did at the other end of the braid. Make sure the knot is right up against the beads to hold the braid securely.

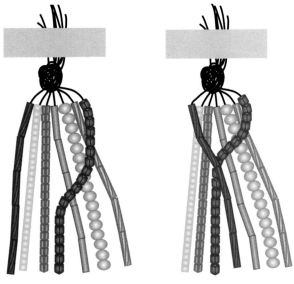

Figure 1   Figure 2

Step 3
Attaching the Cones and Clasp

Thread all seven strands through a gold cone and pull the strands tightly so that the knot and the end of the braid are hidden in the cone. Then thread all seven strands through a clamshell bead tip. Tie a square knot using three strands of the thread for one side and four strands for the other, making sure the knot is all the way inside the clamshell. Clip any excess thread and place a drop of bonding glue onto the knot. Using flat-nosed pliers, squeeze the clamshell shut over the knot. (If you prefer, you may attach the cones using the eye pin method, which is described in Techniques, page 22.) With a round-nose pliers, round off the hook at the end of the clamshell. Attach one end of the clasp with a jump ring. Repeat for the other side of the bracelet.

BARRETTE

MATERIALS

Gold-lined seed beads, size 11°
Pink-white heart seed bead, size 8°
Blue iris twist bugle beads, 1/4" long
Gold AB luster bugle beads, 1/4" long
Pink matte twist bugle beads, 1/4" long
Bronze triangle beads
Matte iris AB triangle beads
1 gold barrette back
Nymo beading thread, black, size B, 7 yards

TOOLS

Beading needle, size 12
Bonding glue

Step 1
Stranding the Beads

Repeat Step 1 of the bracelet instructions, except make the strands 4" long.

Step 2
Braiding the Strands

Repeat Step 2 of the bracelet instructions.

Step 3
Attaching the Braid to the Barrette Back

Cover the barrette back with glue. Tuck the end knots under the braid so they are not visible and lay the braid evenly onto the barrette back. Press and hold for a minute; let sit until dry.

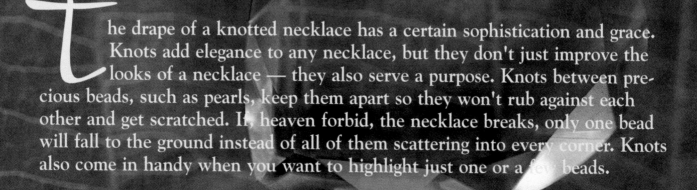

Chapter

4

Knotted Projects

The drape of a knotted necklace has a certain sophistication and grace. Knots add elegance to any necklace, but they don't just improve the looks of a necklace — they also serve a purpose. Knots between precious beads, such as pearls, keep them apart so they won't rub against each other and get scratched. If, heaven forbid, the necklace breaks, only one bead will fall to the ground instead of all of them scattering into every corner. Knots also come in handy when you want to highlight just one or a few beads.

Knotted Pumpkin Bead Choker and Bracelet

String one metal accent bead, one orange melon bead, and one metal accent bead. Tie another overhand knot, making sure it is up tight against the beads. This is the first bead grouping (fig. 2). Start another overhand knot about 2" away from the last knot so that the cord between the knots will measure 1-3/4" after you make the knot. String one metal, one orange, and one metal bead. Tie another overhand knot. (All bead groupings will have approximately 1-3/4" of cord between the knots.) The middle bead grouping is next. Use one metal, one oval wooden bead, and one metal bead. Now do two more orange bead groupings, for a total of five bead groupings; two orange groupings on both sides of the middle wooden bead grouping.

Figure 1

Figure 2

CHOKER

MATERIALS

10 metal accent beads
4 orange melon glass beads, 8mm x 10mm
1 oval painted wooden bead, 15mm x 23mm
2 crimp style cord tips, size to fit your cord
2 silver jump rings
1 silver lobster claw clasp, 15mm
Black satin cord, 2mm (or 1mm if bead holes are
    smaller), 1 yard

TOOLS

Flat-nose or chain-nose pliers

Step 1
Knotting the Beads Onto the Cord
Cut a 1-yard length of cord. Tie an overhand knot about 4" from one end of the cord (fig. 1). Pull snug.

Step 2
Adding the Clasp

Cut the end of the cord 1-3/4" away from the knot on the end bead group. Slip cord tip onto the end of the cord. The end of the cord should be exactly even with the neck of the cord tip (fig. 3). Squeeze the cord tip around the cord with pliers, by folding one flap down flat and then folding the other flap on top of the first one. Then add the lobster claw clasp to the cord tip with a jump ring. Repeat for the other side of the choker. Finished choker measures 16" without the clasp.

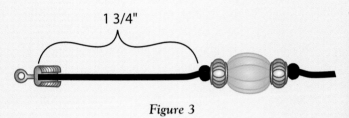

1 3/4"

Figure 3

BRACELET

MATERIALS

6 metal accent beads
2 orange melon glass beads, 8mm x 10mm
1 round painted wooden bead, 16mm
2 crimp style cord tips, size to fit cord
2 silver jump rings
1 silver lobster claw clasp, 10mm
Black satin cord, 2mm (or 1 mm if bead holes are smaller), 1 yard

TOOLS

Flat-nose or chain-nose pliers

Step 1
Knotting the Beads onto the Cord

The bracelet is made the same way as the choker, except it has only three bead groupings: one orange bead group, one round wooden bead group, and one orange bead group. There is a 1" length of cord between the bead groups.

Step 2
Attaching the Cord Tips and Clasp

Repeat Step 2 of choker instructions, except have a 1" length of cord between the bead groups and the clasp ends. The finished bracelet measures 7-1/2" without the clasp.

Change the look of a knotted necklace by using stretchy cord and glass faceted beads.

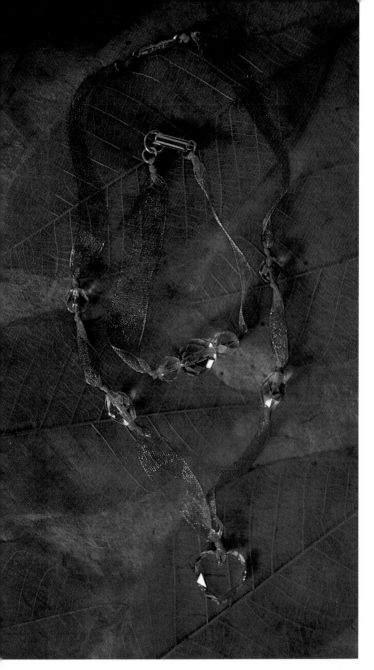

Blue Ribbon Crystal Heart Choker and Bracelet

Step 1
Attaching the Clasp

When using ribbon, cut the end to facilitate bead stringing (fig. 1). Thread the needle with the thin end. String on one side of the clasp and pull it beyond the cut part of the ribbon all the way down the ribbon to the other end, and tie an overhand knot. Bring the knot up close to the clasp before tightening. Trim off the short end of the ribbon to the knot (fig. 2).

Figure 1

CHOKER

MATERIALS

1 crystal heart pendant bead
2 oval faceted crystal beads, 12mm x 9mm
2 round faceted crystal beads, 8mm
1 gold triangle to fit the heart bead
1 gold torpedo clasp
Light blue gossamer ribbon, 1/2" wide, 1 yard

TOOLS

Twisted beading needle
Embroidery scissors
Chain-nose pliers

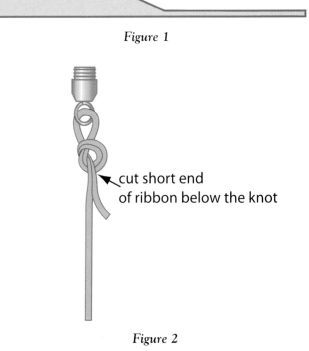

cut short end
of ribbon below the knot

Figure 2

Step 2
Preparing the Heart for Stringing
Open the triangle and fit the open end into the hole in the heart. Carefully squeeze the triangle shut with the pliers.

Step 3
Stringing the Beads
String on one round bead (8mm), one oval bead (12mm x 9mm), the crystal heart, one oval bead (12mm x 9mm), and one round bead (8mm). Make an overhand knot 3" from the clasp. Slide the 8mm bead up to the knot and make another overhand knot, bringing the knot as close to the bead as possible. (See Techniques, page 24, for knot tying instructions.) Make another knot 1" away from the last knot. Slide the oval bead up to the knot and make another knot close to the bead. Slide the heart 2-1/4" away from the knot. Make an overhand knot using both sides of the ribbon, as in Step 1, fig. 2, only do not cut off the ribbon and have the triangle and the heart caught in the loop made by the knot. This will make the heart dangle. Make a knot 2" away from the heart knot. Knot and space the last two beads and clasp to match the first side of the choker.

BRACELET

MATERIALS

1 round faceted crystal bead, 12mm
2 round faceted crystal beads, 8mm
1 gold fold-over clasp
Light blue gossamer ribbon, 1/2" wide, 1 yard

TOOLS

Twisted beading needle
Embroidery scissors

Step 1
Attaching the Clasp
Repeat Step 1 from the choker instructions.

Step 2
Stringing the Beads
String on one of each of the following: an 8mm bead, a 12mm bead, and another 8mm bead. Tie an overhand knot 2-3/4" away from clasp knot. Slide all three beads up against the knot and then tie another overhand knot as close to the beads as possible.

Step 3
Attaching the Other Side of the Clasp
String on other side of the clasp and tie it 2-3/4" away from the last bead knot. Cut off the excess ribbon.

Use smaller ribbon and smaller beads for a different look.

Knotted Pearl Necklace and Anklet

NECKLACE

MATERIALS

1 card Griffen Perlseide No. 4 silk bead thread with
    needle
1 string, 16", of freshwater pearl beads, 4mm
2 bow beads or beads of your choice
1 gold spring ring clasp
2 gold bead tips

TOOLS

Knotting tweezers
Flat-nose pliers
Bonding glue

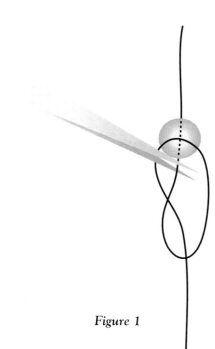

Figure 1

Step 1
Attaching the Bead Tip
Remove the thread from the card and tie two over-hand knots, one right on top of the other at the end of the thread. Cut off the excess thread close to the knots. String on a bead tip, sliding it up to the knots. Apply a drop of glue to the knots, and close the bead tip over the knots with the pliers.

Step 2
Tying the Knots
Tie an overhand knot on the other side of the bead tip. (If this is your first time knotting, practice tying knots as close to a bead as possible before you begin the actual necklace. Note: It is very important to tie the knots as uniformly as possible and to make all the knots go in the same direction. Do not over-tighten the knots, as this tends to make the strand bunch up or buckle.) String on several pearls, and slide one up to the knot next to the bead tip. Tie an overhand knot as close to the pearl as possible. When you are tying an over-hand knot, have the loop of the knot rest in the mid-dle of the bead and hold the thread with the tweezers right under the bead (fig. 1). Pull the thread tight.

Slide another pearl up to the new knot, and make another overhand knot on the other side of that pearl. Repeat the knot-bead-knot pattern until the piece measures 7". String on a bow bead from the top of the bead (fig. 2). Make a knot on the bottom of the bow. Continue adding more pearls and knotting for another 8". String on the other bow bead from the bottom of the bead so the bows are going in opposite directions. Make a knot. String on and knot more pearls for another 7". String on the other bead tip, pushing it close to the last knot and make two over-hand knots inside the bead tip. Cut off the excess thread. Place a drop of glue on the knots in the bead tip, and close the bead tip over the knots with the pliers.

Figure 2

Step 3
Attaching the Clasp

Attach the clasp ends to the bead tips using the instructions from the Techniques section (page 21).

ANKLET

MATERIALS

Griffen Perlseide No. 4 silk bead thread
61 freshwater pearl beads, 4mm
2 bow beads or beads of your choice
2 pearl-like glass seed beads, size 8°
2 gold bead tips
1 gold spring-ring clasp

TOOLS

Knotting tweezers
Flat-nose pliers
Bonding glue

Step 1
Attaching the Bead Tip

Using the silk thread left over from the necklace, attach a bead tip to the end of the thread the same way as in Step 1 of the necklace.

Step 2
Tying the Knots

String on pearls and knot just like in Step 2 of the necklace until piece measures 2-1/2".

Step 3
Making the Dangle

String on a pearl-like seed bead (a seed bead was used here instead of a pearl because the pearls' holes are not big enough for the thread to pass through twice) then string on a bow bead from the top of the bead, and one pearl. *PNBT* the bow bead and the seed bead (fig. 3). Pull thread tight and tie an overhand knot next to the seed bead. There should be two knots above the seed bead: One on the thread going into the bead, and one on the thread as it comes out of the bead. String on pearls and knot just like in Step 2 for 4-1/2". Repeat the instructions for making the dangle, then string on pearls and knot for another 2-1/2".

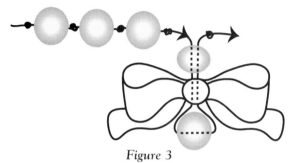

Figure 3

Step 4
Attaching the Bead Tip and the Clasp

String on a bead tip and tie two overhand knots one on top of the other inside the bead tip. Cut off excess thread. Place a drop of glue on the knots in the bead tip and close bead tip over the knots with the pliers. Attach clasp ends to the bead tips following instructions from the technique section.

Chapter

5

Bead Weaving Projects

There are many techniques for weaving beads into glass fabric that can be used to make stunning jewelry. We have included seven bead-weaving techniques in this book — ladder stitch; chevron and daisy chain; horizontal and vertical netting; peyote stitch, flat and tubular; square stitch; and the right angle weave.

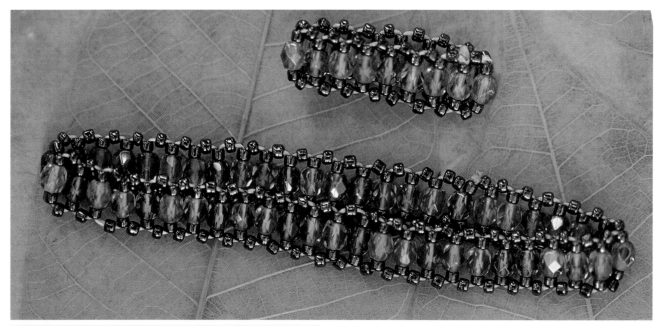

Green Ladder Stitch Bracelet and Ring

BRACELET

MATERIALS

49 faceted Czech fire polished beads in aqua, emerald and peridot, 4mm
Stretchy bead floss, 2 yards
196 hematite Japanese seed beads, size 11° (or any metal color)

TOOLS

2 twisted wire needles

Step 1
Ladder Stitch

Thread a twisted wire needle onto each end of a six-foot length of stretchy bead floss. String on two seed beads, one Czech 4mm bead, and then two more seed beads. Position beads so that they are in the middle of the floss. * Using the left needle, string one seed bead, one Czech bead, and one seed bead. (See fig. 1. We used the three colors of 4mm beads randomly.) Thread the right needle through these three beads going in the opposite direction of the thread already through the beads (fig. 2). Pull both threads tight until all beads fit snugly together. String one seed bead on right needle and one seed bead on left needle. (fig. 3). Push beads down until they touch the other beads. * Repeat between asterisks until bracelet measures 7" or the length to fit your wrist.

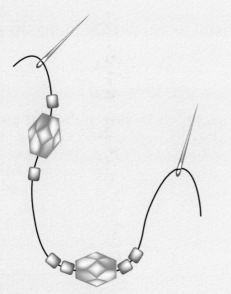

Figure 1

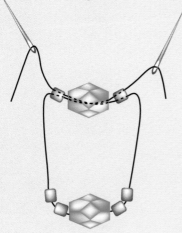

Figure 2

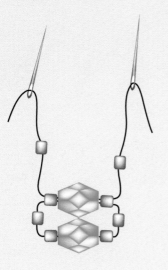

Figure 3

Step 2
Connecting the Ends Together

Bring the ends of bracelet together and insert needles (going in opposite directions) through the two seed beads and the one Czech 4mm bead on the end (the very first beads strung on). Pull both threads tight (fig. 4). To tie the thread ends together, pass the right needle through two seed beads, one Czech 4mm bead and two more seed beads, so that the two thread ends are right next to each other (see red thread on fig. 4). Tie a square knot. Secure knot with glue, slip thread ends into the beads next to the knot, making sure the glue goes into the holes also. Cut off any excess thread and let dry.

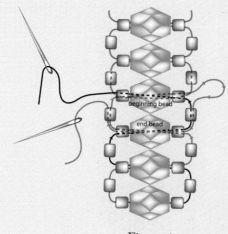

Figure 4

RING

MATERIALS

17 Czech faceted fire polished beads, aqua, emerald, and peridot, 4mm
Stretchy bead floss, 1 yard
68 Japanese seed beads, hematite or any metal color, size 11°

TOOLS

2 twisted wire needles

Step 1
Making the Ring

Repeat Steps 1 and 2 from the bracelet, except make it 2-1/4" long (or length to fit around your finger).

Purple and Black Ladder Stitch Necklace and Earrings

NECKLACE

MATERIALS

91 purple luster hex beads, size 8°
193 silver-lined gold-cut Japanese tubular beads
91 iridescent dark purple seed beads, size 11°
50 black hex bugle beads, 5mm
3 iridescent black faceted teardrop beads, 8mm
1 bronze heart
2 gold bead tips
1 gold barrel clasp
Nymo beading thread, black, size F, 3 yards

TOOLS

2 beading needles, size 12

Step 1
Making the Ladder Stitch Base of the Necklace

Thread needles on each end of a 6-foot length of beading thread. Using one needle, string on one gold, one purple hex, one gold, one dark purple size 11°,

one black bugle bead, one dark purple size 11°, one gold, one purple hex, one gold. Move these beads to the middle of the thread. String on one dark purple size 11°, one black bugle, one dark purple size 11°. Then pass the other needle through the beads in the opposite direction (fig. 1). * Using one of the nee-

Figure 1

dles, string on one gold, one purple hex, one gold. Now use the other needle to string on one gold, one purple hex, one gold. Push these beads down against the other beads. String on one dark purple size 11°, one black bugle bead, one dark purple size 11°. Then pass the other needle through the beads in the opposite direction. * Repeat between the asterisks 16 times or until the piece measures 3-1/2".

Step 2
Creating the First Dangle
With one of the needles, string on two gold beads, 1 faceted teardrop, then one dark purple size 11°, *PNBT* teardrop bead and string on two gold beads (fig. 2). On the other needle, string on two gold beads. Now string on one dark purple size 11°, one black bugle, one dark purple size 11°. Then pass the other needle through the beads in the opposite direction. Repeat between asterisks from Step 1, three times.

Figure 2

Step 3
Creating the Middle Dangle
Using the same needle as the first dangle from Step 2, string on two gold beads, one bugle, one purple hex, one bronze heart, one gold bead, one teardrop, one dark purple size 11°. *PNBT* teardrop, gold bead, heart, purple hex, black bugle, then string on two gold beads (fig. 3). Using the other needle, string on two gold beads. Now string on one dark purple size 11°, one black bugle, one dark purple size 11°. Then pass

Figure 3

the other needle through the beads in the opposite direction. Repeat between asterisks from Step 1 three times.

Step 4
Creating the Third Dangle
Using the same needle as from Steps 2 and 3, create the third dangle by repeating Step 2.

Step 5
Ladder Stitch Base of the Necklace
String on one dark purple size 11°, one black bugle, one dark purple size 11°. Repeat Step 1, between the asterisks, 16 times or until the piece measures 3-1/2".

Step 6
Making One End of the Necklace
String on one gold, one bugle, one dark purple size 11°, one bugle, one gold. Do this on both needles separately. Now thread both needles through * one purple hex bead, one gold bead. * Repeat between asterisks for 1", adjusting length if necessary to fit your neck. Remember to make only half of the adjustment now and the other half on the other end of the necklace.

Step 7
Attaching the Clasp
Attach the bead tip as close to the beads as possible and attach clasp to the bead tip. See Techniques, page 21, for instructions on how to attach bead tip and clasp.

Step 8
Making the Other End of the Necklace
Thread about 3 feet of thread with two needles. Pass one needle through the dark purple size 11°, black bugle and dark purple size 11° at the beginning of the necklace. Center the beads in the middle of the thread and repeat Step 6.

Step 9
Attaching the Other End of the Clasp
Repeat Step 7.

EARRINGS

MATERIALS

2 purple luster hex beads, size 8°
4 silver-lined gold-cut Japanese tubular beads
2 black hex bugle beads, 5mm
2 black iridescent faceted teardrop beads, 8mm
2 iridescent dark purple seed beads, size 11°
2 bronze heart beads
2 gold head pins
2 gold kidney ear wires

TOOLS

Flat-nose pliers
Round-nose pliers

Step 1
Making the Dangles

Put one dark purple size 11° seed bead, one teardrop, one gold, one heart, one purple hex, one bugle, and one gold bead onto a head pin.

Step 2
Attaching the Ear wires

Bend the end of the wire at a 90-degree angle close to the last bead with the flat-nose pliers (fig. 4). Using round nose pliers hold the wire just above the bend and wrap the wire around pliers making a small loop. (fig. 5). Before closing the loop, slip on the earring wire. Cut wire with wire cutters and close the loop with the flat-nose pliers. Repeat Steps 1 and 2 for other earring.

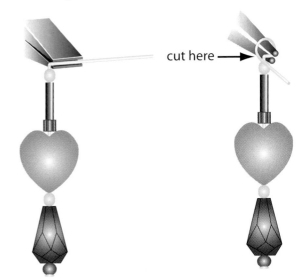

cut here →

Figure 4   *Figure 5*

Blue and Green Chevron Necklace

NECKLACE

MATERIALS

49 light green wonder beads, 4mm
294 metallic green seed beads, size 11°
53 matte cobalt blue seed beads, size 6°
44 blue transparent bi-cone beads, 10mm x 6mm
2 silver clamshell bead tips
1 silver round insert-style clasp
Nymo beading thread, white or light blue, size F, 3 yards

TOOLS

2 beading needles, size 11
Round-nose pliers
Flat-nose pliers

Step 1
Making the Chevron Chain Necklace Base

Thread needle with 2 yards of thread. Leave a 12" tail. String on one wonder bead, one blue bi-cone, one wonder bead, one blue bi-cone, one wonder bead, three metallic beads, one cobalt bead, three metallic beads, and then *PNBT* the first wonder bead strung on, one blue bi-cone, and the next wonder bead. This is the first "stitch" (fig. 1). String three metallic beads, one cobalt, three metallics, one wonder bead, one blue bi-cone. Next *PNT* the third wonder bead strung on from first "stitch." This makes the second "stitch" (fig. 2). String on three metallics, one cobalt, three metallics, one wonder bead, one blue bi-cone. *PNT* wonder bead strung on in the second stitch.

This makes the third "stitch" (fig. 3). Repeat the third "stitch" 40 times, or until piece measures 10-1/2", keeping thread tension tight throughout. Make sure you end with a chevron (both ends look alike with the "V" going up). Tie an overhand knot and weave thread end back through the beads until secure and cut off excess. Do the same thing to the thread tail at the beginning of the necklace.

on the other end of the thread. String on three metallic, one cobalt, three metallic, and one wonder bead, to one of the thread ends and three metallic, one cobalt, three metallic and one wonder bead to the other (fig. 5). Now using both needles at the same time so that both threads go through the beads, string on one cobalt, three metallic, one cobalt, three metallics, one cobalt (fig. 6). Attach a bead tip. Now attach one end of the clasp to the bead tip. Repeat on the other end of the necklace.

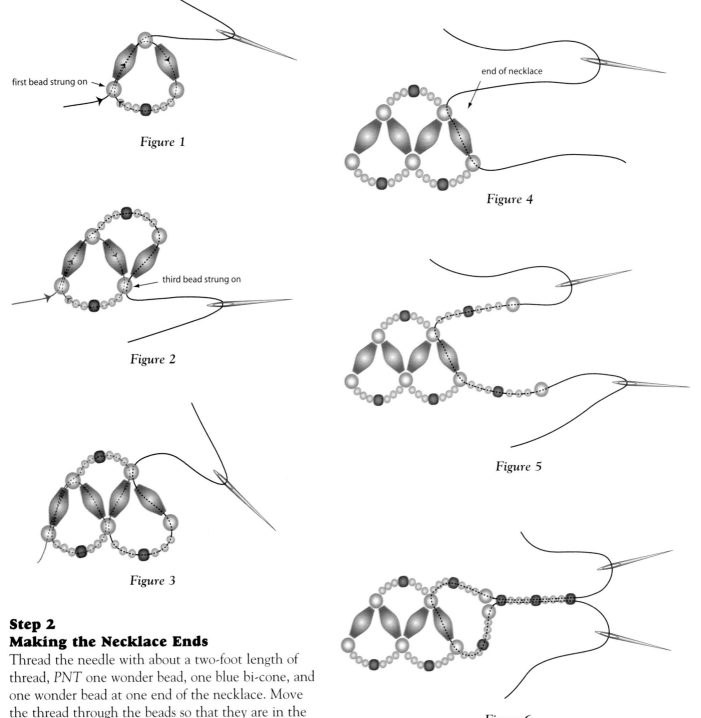

first bead strung on

Figure 1

third bead strung on

Figure 2

Figure 3

end of necklace

Figure 4

Figure 5

Figure 6

Step 2
Making the Necklace Ends
Thread the needle with about a two-foot length of thread, *PNT* one wonder bead, one blue bi-cone, and one wonder bead at one end of the necklace. Move the thread through the beads so that they are in the center of the thread (fig. 4). Thread another needle

EARRINGS

Step 1
Stringing the Beads

Thread a needle with a length of thread about one yard long. String on six metallic beads, one wonder bead, one blue bi-cone, one wonder bead, three metallics, one cobalt, three metallics, one wonder bead, one blue bi-cone, one wonder bead, three metallics, one cobalt, and three metallics. Make sure the beads are in the middle of the thread. *PNBT* the second wonder bead strung on, the first blue bi-cone strung on, and the first wonder bead strung on (fig. 7).

Figure 7

Step 2
Attaching the Ear Wire

PNT the loop on the bottom of the ear wire and *PNBT* the first six metallic beads strung on (fig. 8). *PNBT* beads until thread comes out where the thread went in and make a square knot using both thread ends (fig. 9). Hide the knot in a bead and pass the thread ends through several beads, then cut off the excess.

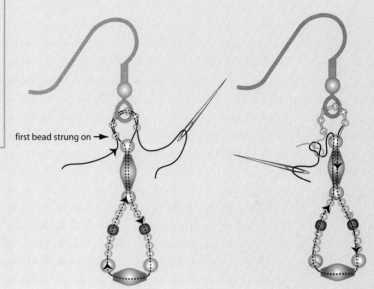

first bead strung on →

Figure 8   **Figure 9**

Using bugle beads in the chevron chain creates a different look.

Purple Chevron Choker and Earrings

CHOKER

MATERIALS

280 lavender seed beads, size 11°
150 silver gray Japanese tubular beads
68 clear AB-finish twist bugle beads, 4mm
3 clear glass faceted teardrop beads, 10mm x 7mm
3 clear glass lantern cut beads, 5mm
1 silver fish hook clasp
2 silver bead tips
White Nymo beading thread, size F, 4-1/2 yards

TOOLS

2 size 12 beading needles
Round nose pliers
Flat nose pliers

Step 1
Chevron Stitch Body of the Choker

Using about 3 yards of thread, string on one silver bead, one bugle, one silver, one bugle, one silver, two lavenders, one silver, and two lavenders. *PNBT* first silver, bugle, and silver beads strung on. Pull tight (fig. 1). This makes the first "stitch." Next string on two lavenders, one silver, two lavenders, one silver, one bugle, then *PNT* the third silver bead strong on the first "stitch." Pull tight (fig. 2). This makes the second "stitch." For "stitch" three, string on two lavender, one silver, two lavender, one silver, one bugle. *PNT* the second silver bead strung on the second "stitch" (fig. 3). Repeat "stitch" three 18 more times for a total of 21 stitches. The next "stitch" is the first dangle stitch. To make the stitch, string on two lavender, one silver, one lavender, one teardrop, one silver, one lantern cut, and one silver. *PNBT* the lantern cut, one silver, one teardrop, one lavender, and one silver. Then string on two lavender, one silver and one bugle. *PNT* the second silver bead strung on from the stitch before (fig. 4). Repeat stitch three 7 times and then you are ready for the middle dangle stitch. String two lavender, one silver, two lavender, one silver, two lavender, one silver, one teardrop, one lavender, one lantern cut, one lavender. *PNBT* the lantern cut, one lavender, one teardrop, one silver, two lavender, one silver, two lavender, and one silver. String on two lavender, one silver, one bugle. *PNT* the second silver bead from the previous stitch. Repeat stitch three 7 times, then repeat the first dangle stitch to make the third dangle. Now finish the chevron body of the choker by repeating stitch three 21 times. Weave in the thread tails on both sides by going *BT* the beads until secure.

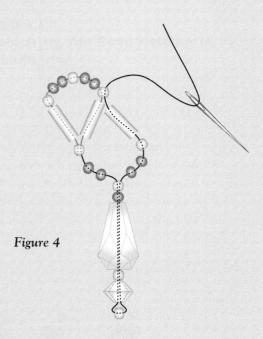

Figure 4

Step 2
Making the Ends of the Choker
Using about 2 feet of thread, *PNT* one silver, one bugle, and one silver bead from the last chevron stitch on the body of the choker. Move the thread through the beads until the beads are in the center of the thread. Thread another needle on the other end of the thread. On the end of the thread coming out of the top edge of the choker string two lavender beads. On the other end of the thread, string two lavender, one silver, two lavender beads (fig. 5). Now string the following beads onto both needles: *one silver, one bugle, one silver, two lavender, one silver, two lavender; * repeat between the asterisks two times then string on one silver, one bugle, and one silver. Attach a bead tip and then attach one end of the clasp to the bead tip (see technique section). Repeat Step 2 for the other end of the choker.

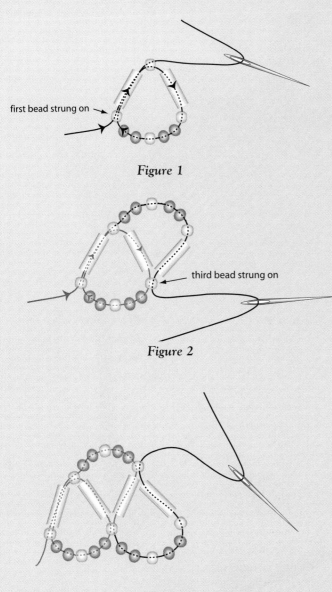

first bead strung on

Figure 1

third bead strung on

Figure 2

Figure 3

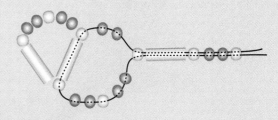

Figure 5

EARRINGS

MATERIALS

6 lavender seed beads, size 11°
6 silver gray Japanese tubular beads
2 clear AB-finish twist bugle beads, 4mm
2 clear glass faceted teardrop beads, 10mm x 7mm
2 clear glass lantern cut beads, 5mm
2 silver fishhook earring wires
2 silver head pins
2 silver jump rings

TOOLS

Flat-nose pliers
Round-nose pliers
Wire cutters

Step 1
Making the Dangle
On a headpin, place the beads in this order: one lantern cut, one lavender, one teardrop, one lavender, one silver, one bugle, one silver and one lavender.

Step 2
Attaching the Earring Wires
Using flat-nose pliers, make a 90-degree bend in the wire close to the last bead. Cut the wire about 1/4" away from the bend, then with round-nose pliers grab the end of the wire and turn the pliers forming the wire into a loop. Attach the earring wire to the dangle using a jump ring. Repeat Steps 1 and 2 for the second earring.

Daisy Chain

Topaz and Lavender Daisy Chain Necklace and Bracelet

NECKLACE

MATERIALS

56 topaz round faceted glass beads, 5mm
1 topaz round faceted glass bead, 7mm
10 gms gold luster amethyst Japanese tubular beads
2 gold bead tips
1 gold barrel clasp
Nymo beading thread, white, size F, 6 yards

TOOLS

Beading needle, size 11
Round-nose pliers
Flat-nose pliers

Step 1
Making the Daisy Chain

Using about 6 yards of thread, string 12 amethyst beads leaving an 8" tail. Make a circle by *PNBT* the first bead strung on (fig. 1). String on one topaz bead (5mm), *PNT* the sixth bead from the first bead strung on (fig. 2). * String on one amethyst, *PNT* adjacent bead on circle, string on one amethyst bead. *PNT* the first bead just strung on (fig. 3). String on 10 amethyst beads, *PNT* the second bead strung on from the two amethysts strung on just before these 10 (fig. 4). String on one topaz bead (5mm), *PNT* the sixth bead strung on.* Repeat between asterisks 25 times.

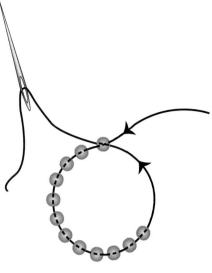

Figure 1

Figure 2

Figure 3

Figure 4

Step 2
Making the Dangle

PNBT the next three beads of the circle so that the needle is coming out of the bottom of the daisy (fig. 5). Make three more daisies; then make a daisy using the 7mm topaz bead and 15 amethyst beads instead of 10. When you are done with the big daisy, *PNBT* the beads of the daisies of the dangle so that the thread is coming out on the opposite side of the top daisy (fig. 6).

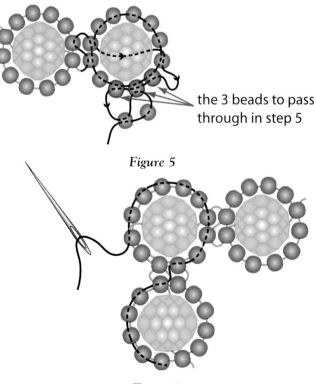

the 3 beads to pass through in step 5

Figure 5

Figure 6

Step 3
Making Second Half of the Necklace
Continue in the daisy chain making 26 more daisies for the other side of the necklace.

Step 4
Attaching the Clasp
Attach bead tips to each end of the necklace and then attach the clasp ends to the bead tips. (See Techniques, page 22.)

BRACELET

MATERIALS

23 topaz round faceted glass beads, 5mm
276 gold luster amethyst Japanese tubular beads
2 gold bead tips
1 gold barrel clasp
Nymo beading thread, white, size F, 4 yards

TOOLS

Beading needle, size 11
Round-nose pliers
Flat-nose pliers

Step 1
Making the Daisy Chain
Make the bracelet the same way as the necklace, but omitting the dangle. This bracelet has 23 daisies.

Step 2
Attaching the Bead Tips and Clasp
Attach the bead tips to the ends of the bracelet and then attach the clasp ends to the bead tips. (See Techniques, page 22.)

Black and Turquoise Triangle Daisy Chain Necklace and Earrings

NECKLACE

> ### MATERIALS
>
> *1 tube of green iridescent Japanese seed beads*
> *180 black seed beads, size 11°*
> *13 turquoise druk beads, 4mm*
> *31 black AB finish druk beads, 4mm*
> *2 silver clamshell bead tips*
> *1 silver lobster claw clasp*
> *Silamide beading thread, black, size A, 3-1/2 yards*
>
> ### TOOLS
>
> *Beading needle, size 12*

Step 1
Attaching One Side of the Clasp
Use about 3-1/2 yards of thread and attach one end of the clasp using a clamshell bead tip. (See Techniques, page 22.)

Step 2
Making the Daisies
*String two black seed beads, then to start the single daisy stitch, string 12 black seed beads. *PNBT* the first bead of the 12, forming a circle. String one turquoise druk bead then *PNT* the sixth bead from the first bead of the circle. Then string two black seed beads, two green seed beads (fig. 1). Next, make the attached daisy stitches. To do this, string 11 green seed beads. *PNBT* the first bead of the 11, then string one black druk bead. *PNT* the fifth bead from the first bead of the circle. String two green seed beads. *PNBT* the fifth and sixth bead of circle, then back through the two beads just strung on (fig. 2). String nine green seed beads. *PNBT* the first bead of the two beads. String one black druk then *PNT* the fifth bead from the first bead of the circle. Pull tight (fig. 3).

Repeat this stitch one more time for a total of three black druk-attached daisy stitches. Then, string on two green beads. * Repeat between the asterisks two more times. String two black seed beads then make one black seed bead turquoise druk daisy. String two black seed beads, two green seed beads. Then make two attached green seed bead black druk daisies, one attached black seed bead and turquoise druk daisy. Then make two more attached green seed bead black druk daisies. String two green seed beads and two black seed beads. Make one more black seed bead turquoise druk daisy. Then, string two black seed beads and two green seed beads.

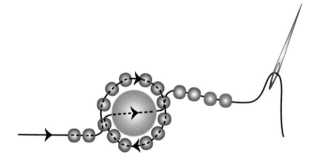

Figure 1

Figure 2

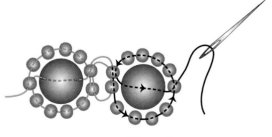

Figure 3

Step 3
Making the Daisy Triangle

Make three attached green seed bead black druk daisies. These will be the top of the triangle. When you finish the third daisy, *PNBT* the beads of the daisy, so that the needle is coming out of the bead next to the two-bead attachment (fig. 4). String two green seed beads. *PNBT* the two beads next to the attachment beads from the third daisy, then *PNBT* the two beads just strung on. String nine green seed beads. *PNT* the first bead of the two-bead attachment. String one black druk bead then *PNBT* the sixth bead of the 11 beads around the druk, and the seventh through the tenth, as well. Then *PNT* seventh and eighth bead from the middle daisy of the top of the triangle then *PNBT* the ninth and tenth bead of the daisy stitch you just made. *PNBT* the eleventh, first, second, third, fourth, fifth, sixth, seventh and eighth beads (fig. 5). String two green seed beads; *PNBT* the seventh and eighth beads, then *PNBT* the two beads just strung on. String nine green seed beads then *PNT* the first bead of the two beads strung on. String one black druk, then *PNT* the sixth bead of beads around druk, and also through the seventh and eighth. *PNT* the seventh and eighth beads of top left hand side daisy, then back through the seventh and eighth beads of the daisy you just made. Then back through the ninth and tenth of the daisy you just made. Then *PNT* beads nine and ten from middle top daisy. Then back through the ninth, tenth, eleventh, first, second and third of the daisy you just made (fig. 6). String two black seed beads, then *PNBT* the second, and third green seed beads. Then back through the two black seed beads. String 10 black seed beads. *PNBT* the first bead of the two attachment black seed beads. String one turquoise druk bead. *PNT* the sixth bead of the seed beads around druk, then *BT* to fifth, fourth, third and second. Next, *PNT* the sixth and fifth beads of middle row right hand side daisy, then *BT* the third and second beads of daisy you just made. Then *PNBT* the sixth, fifth, fourth, third, second, first, and eleventh of middle row right-hand-side daisy. Then through the tenth, ninth, eighth, seventh, and sixth beads of the third top daisy (fig. 7). Now you are done with the triangle.

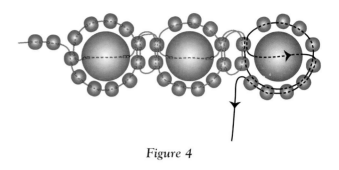

Figure 4

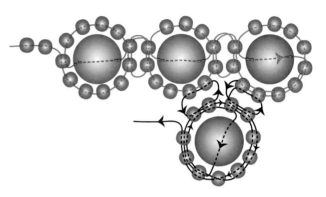

Figure 5

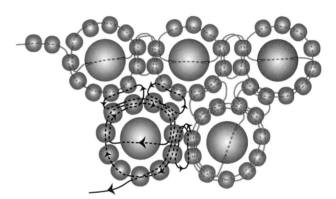

Figure 6

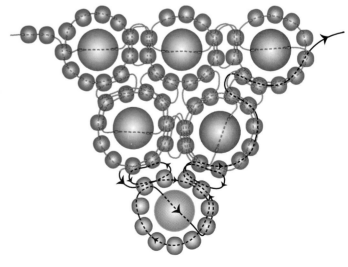

Figure 7

Step 4
Making the Other Half of the Necklace
This side is symmetrical to the other side. Work the same pattern of daisy stitches *backwards*.

Step 5
Attaching the Other Side of the Clasp
String one clamshell bead tip, one seed bead. Tie two or three overhand knots around bead making sure necklace beads are close to bead tip and seed bead is inside clamshell. Cut the excess thread and place a dab of glue over knots. Squeeze clamshell closed and slip other end of clasp over hook of bead tip and turn closed with round nose pliers.

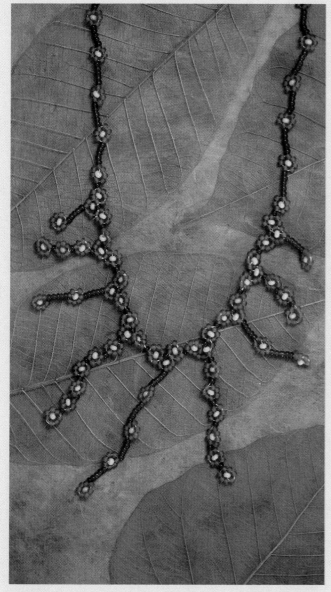

Using size 11° seed beads for the middle of the daisy creates a petite flower.

EARRINGS

MATERIALS
34 black seed beads, size 11°
48 green iridescent Japanese seed beads
Silamide beading thread, black, size A, 2 yards
1 pair of fishhook ear wires

TOOLS
Beading needle, size 12

Step 1
Making the Daisies
String two green seed beads then make two green seed bead black druk attached daisies and one black seed bead turquoise druk attached daisy. *PNBT* three daisies and two seed beads on the top (fig. 8).

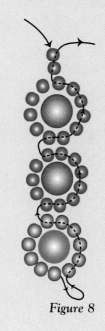

Figure 8

Step 2
Attaching the Ear wire
String five black seed beads. *PNT* the loop of the ear wire, then through the two green seed beads on top of the earring. Pull tight. *PNT* all the seed beads around the first black druk bead and back through the five black seed beads in the ear wire loop. Repeat several times. Cut off any excess thread. Repeat Steps 1 and 2 for the other earring.

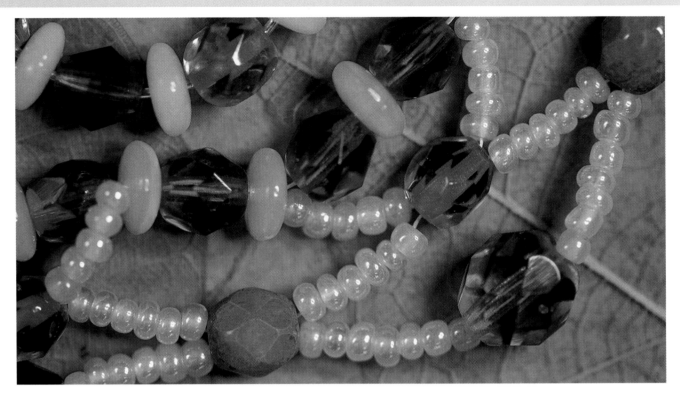

Blue, White, and Purple Netted Choker and Earrings

This choker is made using a horizontal netting technique.

CHOKER

MATERIALS

39 milky white rondelles, 7mm

40 transparent turquoise faceted glass beads, 6mm

9 purple-lined turquoise faceted glass beads, 6mm

8 opaque lavender faceted glass beads, 7mm

4 capri blue lantern-cut faceted glass beads, 6mm

2 light blue lantern-cut faceted glass beads, 5mm

1 transparent turquoise faceted glass bead, 8mm

5 gms pearl white seed beads, size 10°

2 silver clamshell bead tips

1 silver toggle clasp

Nymo beading thread, white, size F, 6 yards

TOOLS

Beading needle, size 11

Embroidery scissors

Round-nose pliers

Flat-nose pliers

Bonding glue

Step 1
Row One

Use about 4 feet of thread and tie a stop bead to the end of the thread with a square knot (fig. 1). String on one transparent turquoise bead (6mm), one rondelle, one transparent turquoise bead (6mm), one rondelle, keeping this pattern for 14-1/2". Tie on another stop bead as close to the beads as possible. Take the needle off of the thread.

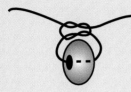

Figure 1

Step 2
Row Two

Thread a new, 2-yard length of thread onto the needle. Tie a stop bead. *PNT* the first 14 beads from Row 1. * String on five white seed beads, one purple-lined turquoise bead, 5 white seed beads. Skip the next turquoise bead, rondelle and one other turquoise bead from Row 1, then *PNT* one rondelle, one turquoise, one rondelle from Row 1 (fig. 2). * Repeat between asterisks eight times. On the last repeat, instead of *PNT* the one rondelle, one turquoise, one rondelle, *PNT* the last 14 beads of the first row. Tie on a stop bead.

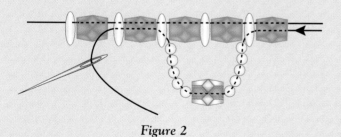

Figure 2

Step 3
Row Three

Using a new 4-foot length of thread, *PNT* the first 14 beads from Row 1 and the five white seed beads and one purple-lined turquoise bead from Row 2. String on six white seed beads, one lavender bead, and six white seed beads. *PNT* purple-lined turquoise bead from Row 2. Repeat between the asterisks seven

times. On last repeat, *PNT* purple-lined bead and five white seed beads from Row 2 and the last 14 beads from Row 1.

Step 4
Row Four

Thread a new 4-foot length of thread. Tie a stop bead. *PNT* the first 14 beads from Row 1, through five white seed beads and one purple-lined bead from Row 2, and six white seed beads and one lavender bead from Row 3. * String on six white seed beads, one light blue bead, six white seed beads. *PNT* one lavender bead from Row 3. * Repeat between asterisks two times except instead of one light blue bead, string on one capri blue bead each time. String seven white seed beads, one turquoise bead (8mm), and seven white seed beads. *PNT* the lavender bead from Row 3. Finish the row to match the first half of the row with two capri blue beads and one light blue bead. *PNT* the lavender bead, six white seed beads from Row 3, one purple-lined bead and five white seed beads from Row 2 and remaining 14 beads from Row 1. Tighten all strings.

Step 5
Attaching the Clasp

Remove all stop beads from one side of the choker. Using all strands string on a bead tip. Tie an overhand knot in the bead tip and while tightening the knot push the bead tip as close to the beads as possible. Cut off excess thread and place a drop of glue on the knot and squeeze the bead tip closed with the flat-nose pliers. Using round-nose pliers, close the bead tip hook over the loop on one end of the clasp. Repeat on other side of the choker.

EARRINGS

MATERIALS

8 milky white rondelles, 7mm
2 purple-lined turquoise faceted glass beads, 6mm
4 capri blue lantern cut faceted glass beads, 6mm
4 light blue lantern cut faceted glass beads, 5mm
12 pearl white seed beads, size 10°
1 pair silver hoop ear wires

TOOLS

Flat-nose pliers

Step 1
Stringing the Beads

Onto one hoop earring wire, place three white seed beads, one light blue bead, one rondelle, one capri blue, one rondelle, one purple-lined bead, one rondelle, one capri blue, one rondelle, one light blue,

three white seed beads. With pliers, bend up the end of the hoop so it will fit into the loop of the hoop (fig. 3). Repeat for other earring.

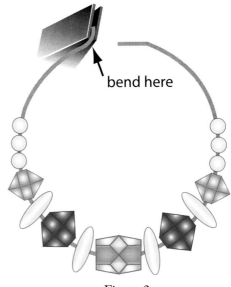

bend here

Figure 3

Vertical Net Necklace and Headband

Don't let the length of these instructions fool you. This project is quick and easy. Vertical netting is a simple technique.

NECKLACE

MATERIALS

1 copper "S" hook and eye clasp
2 strands, 18", charlotte blue iris beads, size 8°
3 blue iris floret beads
12 teardrop (glass) copper iris beads, 8mm x 6mm
50 druk (glass) copper iris beads, 4mm
Nymo beading thread, black, size F, 4 yards

TOOLS

Beading needle, size 12

Step 1
Making the Base Strand

Using about 4 yards of thread, tie a charlotte stop bead leaving a 12" tail, then string on 191 charlottes, for a total of 192 beads. The base strand should measure about 15" and, with a 1" clasp, the finished necklace should measure about 16". Now attach one end of the clasp by wrapping the thread around the clasp loop about six times. Pull tight so that the beads are tight against the clasp and tie a double-half hitch knot. PNBT 47 charlottes and now you are ready to begin Row 1.

Step 2
Row 1

Downward side:
String one druk, five charlottes, one druk, five charlottes, one druk, one charlotte, and one teardrop. *PNBT* one charlotte and one druk.

Upward side:
String five charlottes, one druk, five charlottes. *PNT* the first druk bead from downward side of row and then *PNT* the next seven charlottes on the base strand (fig. 1).

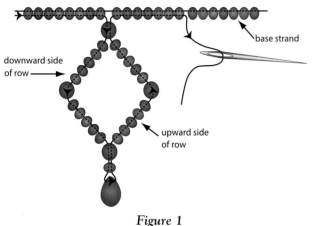

downward side of row →

← upward side of row

base strand

Figure 1

Step 3
Row 2

Downward side:
String one druk, five charlottes. *PNT* the druk bead from upward side of previous row, string five charlottes, one druk, one charlotte, one teardrop. *PNBT* one charlotte, one druk.

Upward side:
String five charlottes, one druk, five charlottes. *PNT* the first druk bead from downward side of the row and then *PNT* the next seven charlottes on the base strand (fig. 2).

Figure 2

Step 4
Rows 3-6

Same as Row 2.

Step 5
Row 7

Same as Row 2–except at the end of the downward side of the row, instead of stringing on a teardrop, string one druk, one charlotte, one floret, one druk, one charlotte. *PNBT* one druk, one floret, one charlotte and one druk (fig. 3). Finish the row same as Row 2.

Figure 3

Step 6
Row 8

Same as Row 7 (except for the dangle beads). String one druk, one charlotte, one druk, one charlotte, one druk, one charlotte, one floret, one druk, one charlotte. *PNBT* one druk, one floret, one charlotte, one druk, one charlotte, one druk, one charlotte, one druk (fig. 4). Now finish the row the same as Row 7.

Figure 4

Step 7
Row 9
Same as Row 7.

Step 8
Rows 10-15
Same as Row 2. At the end of Row 15, instead of passing the needle through seven charlottes on the base strand, tie a small knot and weave thread end into beadwork until secure. Cut off the excess thread.

Step 9
Attach Other End of the Clasp
Thread needle onto tail of thread at the end of the piece. String on the clasp end. Wrap thread about six times around the loop, and pull tight so beads are against the clasp. Tie a double-half hitch knot. Weave the excess thread through beads until secure and cut off any remaining thread.

HEADBAND

MATERIALS

4 strands, 18″, of blue iris charlotte seed beads,
   size 8°
67 druk (glass) copper iris beads, 4mm
5 blue iris floret beads
12 teardrop (glass) copper iris beads, 8mm x 6mm
1 plastic tortoise shell headband
Nymo beading thread, black, size F, 4-1/2 yards

TOOLS

Beading needle, size 12

Step 1
Making the Base Strand
Use about 4-1/2 yards of black thread. String one size 8° charlotte stop bead, then string on 191 charlottes for a base strand with a total of 192 charlotte beads. Now make one end bead dangle by stringing one copper druk bead, one charlotte, one floret, one druk, and one charlotte. *PNBT* one druk, one floret, one charlotte, one druk, and 47 charlottes. Now you are ready to begin Row 1.

Step 2
Row 1
Downward side:
String one druk bead, five charlottes, one druk, five charlottes, one druk, one charlotte, and one copper teardrop. *PNBT* one charlotte and one druk.

Upward side:
String five charlottes, one druk, five charlottes. *PNT* the first druk bead from the downward side of row, and then *PNT* the next seven charlottes on the base strand.

Step 3
Row 2
Downward side:
String 1 druk, five charlottes. *PNT* last druk bead from upward side of previous row. String five charlottes, one druk, one charlotte, one teardrop. *PNBT* one charlotte and one druk.

Upward side:
String five charlottes, one druk, five charlottes. *PNT* the first druk bead from downward side of the row and then *PNT* the next seven beads on the base strand.

Step 4
Rows 3 and 4
Repeat Row 2.

Step 5
Row 5
Downward side:
String one druk, five charlottes. *PNT* the druk bead from the upward side of the previous row. String five charlottes, one druk, five charlottes, one druk, five charlottes, one druk, one charlotte, one teardrop. *PNBT* one charlotte, one druk.

Upward side:
String five charlottes, one druk, five charlottes. *PNT* the second druk bead strung on the downward side of the row. String five charlottes, one druk, five charlottes. *PNT* first druk from the downward side of the row. *PNT* the next seven beads of the base strand (fig. 5).

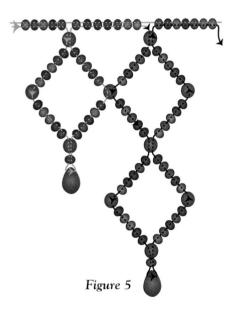

Figure 5

Step 6
Row 6
Downward side:
String one druk, five charlottes. *PNT* the druk bead from upward side of previous row (second one strung on upward portion of row). String five charlottes, one druk, one charlotte, one teardrop. *PNBT* one charlotte and one druk.

Upward side:
String five charlottes, one druk, five charlottes. *PNT* corresponding druk from the downward side of the row. String five charlottes, one druk, five charlottes. *PNT* the first druk strung on from the downward side of the row. *PNT* the next seven beads of the base

strand (fig. 6).

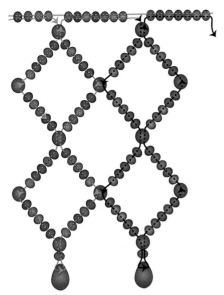

Figure 6

Step 7
Row 7
Row 7 is the same as Row 6 except at the end of the downward side of the row, where instead of stringing on a teardrop, string one floret, one druk, one charlotte, then *PNBT* one druk, one floret, one charlotte and one druk (fig. 7). Finish the row the same as Row 6.

Figure 7

Step 8
Row 8
Row 8 is the same as Row 7 except for the dangle beads. String one druk, one charlotte, one druk, one charlotte, one druk, one charlotte, one floret, one druk, one charlotte. *PNBT* one druk, one floret, one charlotte, one druk, one charlotte, one druk, one charlotte, one druk. Now finish the row the same as Row 7.

Step 9
Row 9
Same as Row 7.

Step 10
Rows 10 and 11
Same as Row 6.

Step 11
Rows 12, 13, 14, 15
Same as Row 2.

Step 12
Making the End Dangle
At the end of Row 15, *PNT* the 47 charlottes on the end of the base strand. Now string one druk, one charlotte, one floret, one druk, and one charlotte. *PNBT* one druk, one floret, one charlotte, one druk and 97 base strand charlottes, so the needle is coming out of the middle of the base strand.

Step 13
Attaching the Bead Netting to the Headband
Find the center of the plastic headband and place the base strand along the top of headband, matching centers. Wrap thread around headband between teeth and *PNT* three beads from base strand. Wrap thread around the headband between the next teeth and then through next three beads of base strand. Repeat until you reach the last tooth on the headband. *PNBT* the base strand beads until you reach the center of the headband. Attach the other side of the netting to the headband in the same manner.

Peyote Stitch Bracelet and Barrette

BRACELET

MATERIALS

5 gms gold-cut silver-lined Japanese tubular beads
5 gms ruby semi-matte silver-lined Japanese tubular beads
5 squash-colored Japanese tubular beads
5 medium green Japanese tubular beads
5 sapphire Japanese tubular beads
6 opaque rose Japanese tubular beads
Nymo beading thread, red, size F, 2 yards
1 gold spring ring clasp

TOOLS

Beading needle, size 12
Embroidery scissors

Step 1
Peyote Stitch

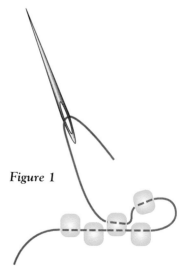

Figure 1

Thread the needle with 6 feet of thread. Leaving a 6" tail, string on five gold beads. *PNBT* the third bead strung on. (fig. 1.) String one gold bead, *PNBT* the first bead strung on. This makes the first two rows. (Follow the design chart for the colors of beads used. Read the chart from bottom to top, working right to left then on the next row left to right.)

For Row 3, string one bead *PNT* last bead from the previous row, string one bead then *PNT* the first bead from the previous row. Each row has two beads in it. Continue in this manner, repeating the design chart when necessary until the piece measures 6-3/4", ending with a pink bead and a red parallelogram. Finish off with two rows of gold beads so that each end of the bracelet is the same.

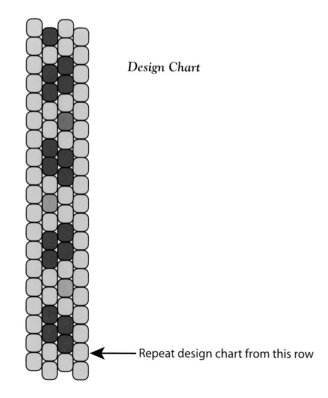

Design Chart

← Repeat design chart from this row

Step 2
Attaching the Clasp

With the remaining thread string on six gold beads and one end of the clasp. *PNBT* the beads of the last two rows of the peyote then back through the six gold beads, pulling tightly. Do this two or three more times, then tie a knot and weave the thread end through the beads until secure. Cut off the excess thread. (fig. 2.) Using the 6" tail of thread from the beginning of the bracelet, repeat Step 2.

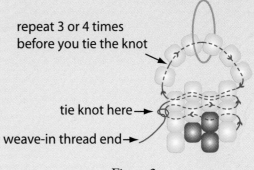

repeat 3 or 4 times
before you tie the knot

tie knot here →

weave-in thread end →

Figure 2

BARRETTE

MATERIALS

205 gold-cut silver-lined Japanese tubular beads
36 ruby semi-matte silver-lined Japanese tubular beads
2 squash-colored Japanese tubular beads
2 medium green Japanese tubular beads
2 sapphire Japanese tubular beads
2 opaque rose Japanese tubular beads
Nymo beading thread, red, size F, 1 yard
1 gold barrette finding, 2"

TOOLS

Beading needle, size 12
Embroidery scissors
Bonding glue

Step 1
Peyote Stitch

Make another strip of peyote stitches as you did in Step 1 of the bracelet, only make this strip 2-1/2" long.

Step 2
Making the Fringe

PNBT the second bead down and *PT* four beads and come out through the third bead down on the opposite side. Now string on four gold beads, *PNT* the sixth bead from the top and through four beads to the third bead of the other side. (fig. 3.) Repeat until there are three or four rows left. Weave in the thread ends until secure. Cut off the excess thread.

Step 3
Gluing On the Peyote Strip

Place glue on the peyote strip and then put it onto the barrette finding, folding the ends of the peyote strip over the edges of the barrette. Let dry. If you want two barrettes, repeat Steps 1-3.

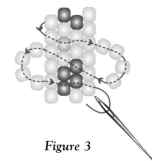

Figure 3

Tubular Peyote Sunset Bracelet and Earrings

BRACELET

MATERIALS

5 gm yellow seed beads, size 11°
5 gm yellow-orange seed beads, size 11°
5 gm orange seed beads, size 11°
5 gm red-orange seed beads, size 11°
5 gm red seed beads, size 11°
5 gm dark red seed beads, size 11°
2 red accent beads
1 gold spring ring clasp
Silamide beading thread, size A, 3 yards

TOOLS

Beading needle, size 12

Step 1
Tubular Peyote

Using about 3 yards of beading thread, string six yellow beads. Leave a 12" tail to use to attach the clasp later. PNBT the first yellow bead strung on forming a circle. These six beads will form Rounds 1 and 2 (fig. 1).

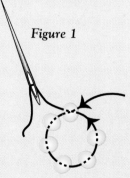

Figure 1

Keep the circle tight by holding the tail of thread.

You will have three beads for each round. (This is called even-count tubular peyote because you start with an even number of beads, but the beads-per-round ends up being an odd number.)

Round 3

String one yellow bead, skip a bead from the bead circle, *PNT* the next bead from the bead circle (fig. 2). String one yellow bead, skip a bead, *PNT* next bead (fig. 3). String one yellow bead, skip a bead, *PNT* next bead. *PNBT* the first bead from this round, so that the needle is properly positioned for the next round. Pull tight.

Round 4

After this round, it will be easy to identify which three beads are on each round. Three of the beads will be definitely higher than the three from the previous row.* String one yellow bead. *PNT* the next stepped-up bead. * Repeat between asterisks two times. Then, *PNBT* the first bead of the Round so that the needle is positioned properly for the next round. Pull tight. Do 3/4" of tubular peyote with the yellow beads, then change to yellow-orange beads for 1/2", orange for 1/2", red-orange for 1/2", red for 1/2", dark red for 1/2", red for 1/2", red-orange for 1/2", orange for 1/2", yellow-orange for 1/2", and yellow for 3/4". (13 rounds equal about 1/2" and 17 rounds equal about 3/4".)

Figure 2

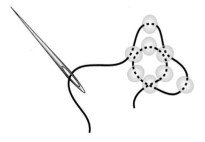

Figure 3

Step 2
Attaching the Clasp

When you are done with the last yellow round of the tubular peyote, string one red accent bead. Then string thread through the loop of the clasp. *PNBT* the red bead then through one of the yellow beads from the last row of the bracelet. Pull tight. *PNBT* red bead, loop of clasp, *BT* red bead then through the next yellow bead from the last row of the bracelet.

Pull tight. Repeat several more times using a different yellow bead from the last row each time. Now *PNBT* the peyote stitches until thread is secure and cut off the excess thread. Repeat for the other end of the bracelet.

EARRINGS

MATERIALS

5 gm yellow seed beads, size 11°
5 gm yellow-orange seed beads, size 11°
5 gm orange seed beads, size 11°
5 gm red-orange seed beads, size 11°
5 gm red seed beads, size 11°
5 gm dark red seed beads, size 11°
2 red accent beads
1 pair gold fishhook ear wires
Silamide beading thread, size A, 3 yards

TOOLS

Beading needle, size 12

Step 1
Tubular Peyote

Repeat Step 1 of the bracelet except change colors as follows: seven rounds of yellow beads, five rounds yellow-orange, five rounds orange, five rounds red-orange, five rounds red, five rounds dark red, five rounds red, five rounds red-orange, five rounds orange, five rounds yellow-orange, seven rounds yellow.

Step 2
Attaching the Ear Wires

String one red accent bead then string six dark red beads. *PNT* ear wire loop then *PNBT* red accent bead and pull tight. *PNT* one of the yellow beads from the last row. *PNBT* red accent bead and all six dark red beads holding on the ear wire. *PNBT* the red accent bead. Then *PNT* next yellow bead from the last row. Repeat one more time. Now weave thread through yellow beads until secure and cut off excess thread. Next you thread the needle onto the tail on the other end of the tubular peyote. *PNT* red accent bead, all six red beads, back through red accent bead, through one yellow bead from Row 1. Pull tight. Repeat two more times then weave tail into yellow beads until secure and clip off any excess. Repeat Steps 1 and 2 for the other earring.

Changing bead color and adding dangles can enhance the tubular peyote bracelet.

Square Stitch Scarab Choker and Belt

Make two squares of scarab square stitch, one 1" x 1-5/8" and one 1-1/2" x 1-5/8" and you can create two totally different projects: a lovely choker necklace and a belt buckle cover for your web belt.

CHOKER

MATERIALS

3 transparent light blue seed beads, size 5°
2 dark green round beads, 7mm
10 black Japanese tubular beads, 1.5mm
82 silver-lined gold-cut Japanese tubular beads,
    1.5mm
86 pink luster light olive Japanese tubular beads,
    1.5mm
88 metallic teal iris Japanese tubular beads, 1.5mm
209 opaque light blue Japanese tubular beads,
    1.5mm
1 silver neck wire
Nymo beading thread, black, size F, 4 yards

TOOLS

Beading needle, size 11 or 12

Step 1
Square Stitch

Using about 4 yards of thread, string on 19 light blue Japanese tubular beads. This is the first row.
For all other rows, string two light blue tubular beads, then *PNT* (in the opposite direction of Row 2) second-to-last bead from Row 1 and then back through the second bead just strung on (fig. 1). String one light blue Japanese tubular bead. *PNT* (in the opposite direction of Row 2) third bead from Row 1, and then back through the bead just strung on. Continue in this manner, stringing on one bead at a time, until the end of the row. Remember to make a two-bead stitch at the beginning of each row. Use the design

chart and continue in the square stitch until finished. Read the chart from left to right and right to left, up from the bottom of the chart to the top.

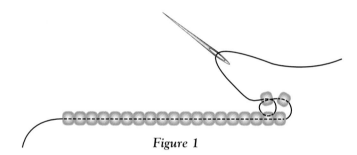

Figure 1

Step 2
Attaching Scarab to the Neck Wire

Pick three light blue size 5° seed beads by making sure the hole is large enough to fit onto the neck wire with room to spare for thread. If you have excess thread left over at the end of the design chart, use it to sew on the beads; if not, get new thread securing end of thread in the beads already worked. Sew the beads onto the square stitched scarab by following fig. 2. Wrap the thread through the beads two or three times. Secure the thread end into the already worked beads and cut off excess. Unscrew the ball at the end of the neck wire. Put on one dark green round bead, the three light blue beads sewn onto the scarab and then one more dark green bead. Slide the beads to the center of the neck wire and screw the ball back on.

last row →

weave-in thread end

Figure 2

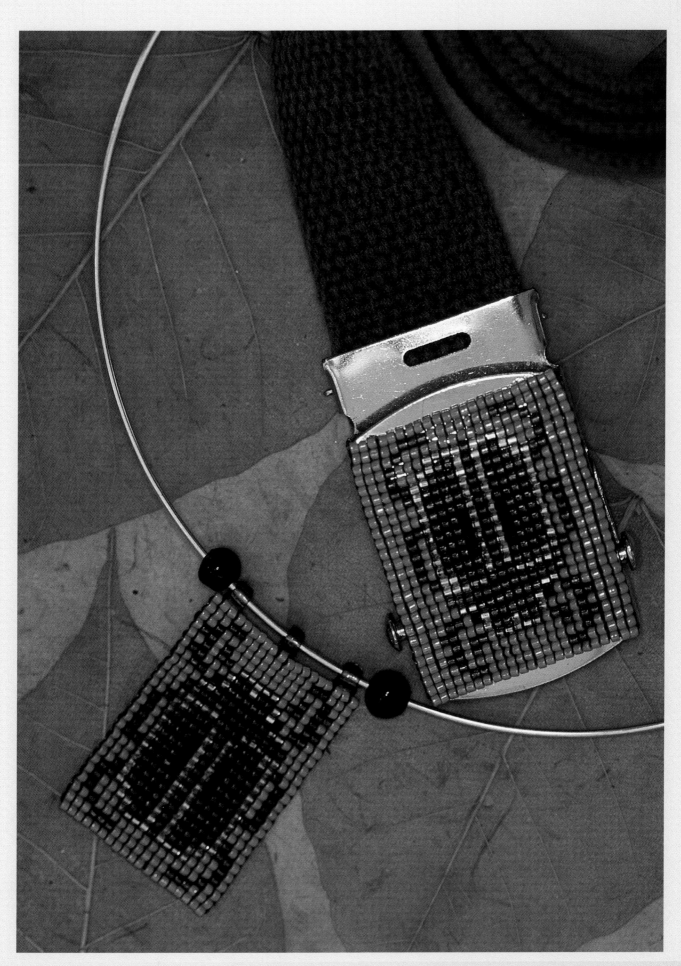

black

metallic teal iris

opaque light blue

pink luster light olive

silver lined gold cut

Design Chart for Scarab Choker

Design Chart for Belt

 black
metallic teal iris
opaque light blue
pink luster light olive
silver lined gold cut

BELT

MATERIALS

10 black Japanese tubular beads, 1.5mm
82 silver-lined gold-cut Japanese tubular beads,
   1.5mm
86 pink luster light olive Japanese tubular beads,
   1.5mm
88 metallic teal iris Japanese tubular beads, 1.5mm
309 opaque light blue Japanese tubular beads,
   1.5mm
1 brown webbed belt and metal buckle
Nymo beading thread, black, size F, 4-1/2 yards

TOOLS

Beading needle, size 11 or 12
Bonding glue

Step 1
Square Stitch

String on 23 light blue Japanese tubular beads for the
first row. Then, following the Scarab Belt design
chart, work in the square stitch (same as Step 1 on
the choker).

Step 2
Gluing the Square Stitch Scarab to the Belt Buckle

Using the bonding glue, glue the beads to the top of
the metal belt buckle. Let dry.

Square Stitch Flower Broach and Earrings

The broach and the earrings are made in exactly the same manner, except that the middle bead on the broach is larger than the middle bead of the earrings. And, of course, the earring flowers are glued to ear studs, and the broach flower is glued to a pin back.

BROACH AND EARRINGS

MATERIALS

90 white iridescent seed beads, size 11°
210 pearly lavender seed beads, size 11°
150 rose lilac seed beads, size 11°
90 bluish-purple seed beads, size 11°
9 kelly green translucent seed beads, size 11°
3 gold seed beads, size 11°
9 green leaf-shaped beads
1 yellow faceted glass bead, 4mm
2 yellow faceted glass beads, 3mm
1 small gold bar pin

1 pair of gold flat pad ear studs
1 pair of comfort clutch earring backs
Green felt
Nymo beading thread, white, size B (or the size to fit
    bead holes), 30 yards

TOOLS

Beading needle, size 12
Bonding glue

Step 1
Making the Petals for the Earrings and the Broach

Thread the needle on about 2 yards of thread. Using the square stitch (see Techniques, page 28, How to Make Square Stitch) and the design chart (Row 1 being on the bottom of the chart and Row 6 on top), make a petal. Increase on both ends of Rows 2 and 3, and decrease on both ends of Rows 5 and 6. Repeat four times for a total of five petals. Leave one yard-long thread end on one of the petals. Weave all the other thread ends into the petals. Each flower has five petals. This project needs three flowers so make ten more petals for the two earrings. Set aside.

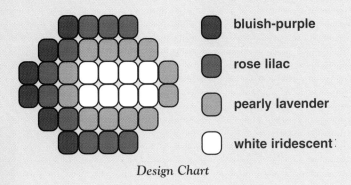

■	bluish-purple
■	rose lilac
■	pearly lavender
□	white iridescent

Design Chart

will be floppy, but that is okay. Arrange the petals so that they overlap and form them into a tight circle (fig. 2). Then, holding them carefully in order, sew the petals in place by passing the needle between the beads (not through the beads) and catch the threads. Keep sewing the petals, one on top of the other, until they are fairly secure. Then pass the needle up through a bead in the middle of the petals and string on one yellow faceted bead (4mm for the broach and 3mm for the earrings) then string on one gold seed bead and *PNBT* the yellow faceted bead and back down through the bead in the middle of the petals and out the back of the flower.

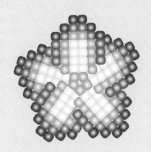

Figure 2

Step 3
Sewing On the Leaves

String on a leaf bead, one green seed bead, then *PNBT* the leaf bead. Attach to the backside of one of the petals by *PNT* one of the beads of the petal, making sure the leaf bead shows through two of the petals (fig. 3). It doesn't have to be too secure, because when you glue the flower to the felt the leaves will be held in place by the glue. Repeat two more times.

Step 2
Sewing the Petals Together

Use the 1 yard-long thread end to sew the petals together. Take five petals and sew them loosely together into a circle by passing needle through the bottom lavender beads of each petal. (See fig. 1.) It

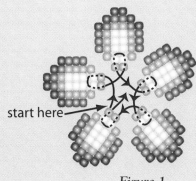

start here →

Figure 1

Figure 3

Step 4
Glue Flower to Felt

Cut a small circle of green felt about 5/8" diameter for the earrings and about 1" in diameter for the broach. Put glue on back of flower and glue it to the felt circle. Make sure you arrange the petals and leaves the way you want them to look. Let dry. Then glue the flower and the felt to the bar pin back or the flat pad earring stud (fig. 4). Let dry. On these earrings you must use the earring backs with the large plastic circle around them, because the earrings are heavy and will droop if the backs are the small kind.

Figure 4

Crystal Right Angle Weave
Pink and Purple Bracelet
and Earrings

Bracelet

MATERIALS

24 pink Swarovski crystals, 6mm
75 purple Swarovski crystals, 3mm
2 silver clamshell bead tips
1 silver lobster claw clasp
Nymo beading thread, black or purple, size F,
3 yards
2 seed beads, size 11°

TOOLS

Beading needle, size 12
Flat-nose pliers
Round-nose pliers
Bonding glue

Step 1
Right Angle Weave

Use about 3 yards of thread. String on four purple crystals, leaving a thread tail about 12" long to be used later for attaching the clasp. *PNBT* the first three crystals strung on, forming a circle (fig. 1). This

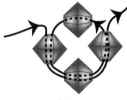

Figure 1

circle forms the first purple "stitch." * String three purple crystals and *PNBT* the end crystal of the previous stitch and back through the first two crystals strung on (fig. 2). *Repeat between the asterisks one time, then * string one pink, one purple, one pink. This forms the pink-purple stitch. *PNBT* end bead of previous stitch and back through the first and second

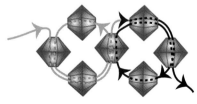

Figure 2

beads strung on (fig. 3). * Repeat between asterisks one time. This forms the "flower." Repeat the three purple stitches, two pink-purple stitches pattern five more times for a total of six "flowers." Add three more purple stitches to the end.

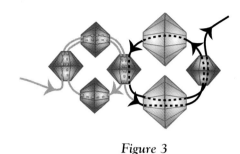

Figure 3

Step 2
Attaching the Clasp

Thread the needle through the clamshell bead tip and string on one seed bead. Pull the bead tight into the bead tip and tie several knots around the seed bead. Place a drop of glue over the knots and bead, and squeeze the clamshell bead tip closed with pliers. Slip clasp loop onto bead tip hook and close hook with round-nose pliers. Repeat Step 2 on the other end of the bracelet.

Earrings

MATERIALS

8 pink Swarovski crystals, 6mm
24 purple Swarovski crystals, 3mm
2 silver clamshell bead tips
1 pair silver lever-back ear wires
2 seed beads, size 11°
Beading thread of your choice, black or purple, size
    F, 2 yards

TOOLS

Beading needle, size 12
Flat-nose pliers
Round-nose pliers
Bonding glue

Step 1
Right Angle Weave

Use about 1 yard of thread leaving a 6" tail and make three purple stitches and two pink-purple stitches. Next *PNBT* the stitches so that the thread is coming out of the same bead as the thread tail (fig. 4).

Step 2
Attaching the Earring Wire

String both thread ends through a clamshell bead tip and one of the ends through a seed bead. Tie a square knot around the seed bead and pull tight, making sure that the knot and seed bead are snugly in the bead tip (fig. 4). Place a drop of glue on the knot and seed bead. Using flat-nose pliers, squeeze clamshell shut. Slip the ear wire loop onto the bead tip hook and close with round-nose pliers. Repeat Steps 1 and 2 for the other earring.

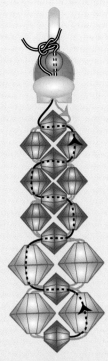

Figure 4

Blue and Roses
Right Angle Weave
Dog Collar and Ring

Dog Collar

MATERIALS

322 light blue druk beads, 4mm

16 light green druk beads, 4mm

8 pink druk beads, 4mm

1 blue olive shaped luster bead with a rose,
18mm x 13mm

1 blue round luster bead with a rose, 10mm

Nymo beading thread, blue (or color of your choice),
size F, 3-1/2 yards

TOOLS

Beading needle, size 11

Step 1
Row 1

Use about 3 yards of thread and leave a 12" tail. String on four light blue druk beads. *PNBT* the first three beads strung on. This forms the first stitch. String on three more blue druk beads and *PNT* the end bead of the first stitch and back through the first two beads strung on. This forms the second stitch (fig. 1). Make eight more stitches using blue druk

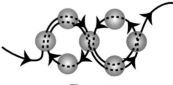

Figure 1

beads. Then make one stitch stringing on in this order: one green druk and two blue. For the next stitch, string on two blue and one green. * Make six more all-blue bead stitches, then one green, two blue, and then one stitch of two blue and one green. * Repeat between asterisks two times, then make 10 all-blue bead stitches.

Step 2
Row 2
PNT the top bead of last stitch from Row 1. String on three blue beads. *PNBT* top bead from Row 1 and then *PNBT* the first of the three beads strung on. This is the first stitch of Row 2. String on two blue beads. *PNT* top bead of the next stitch from Row 1. Then *PNBT* the end bead of the previous stitch and both beads just strung on. This is the second stitch of Row 2. Then *PNT* the top bead of the stitch from Row 1 and string on two blue beads. *PNT* end bead of previous stitch, next top bead from Row 1 and through the first bead strung on. This is the third stitch of Row 2 (fig. 2). Make seven more all-blue bead stitches. * For the next stitch, string one pink bead and one green bead. Then for the next stitch, string one green bead and one blue bead. Next make six all-blue bead stitches. * Repeat between asterisks three times, then make four more all-blue bead stitches.

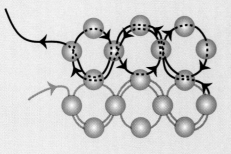

Figure 2

Step 3
Row 3
Using right angle weave stitch, make 46 all blue stitches.

Step 4
Making the Loop End of the Clasp
Pass the thread through the end beads until the thread comes out of the end bead of the middle row. String on 12 blue beads and *PNBT* the first bead of the 12, forming a loop (fig. 3). Weave thread back through some of the stitches until secure and then cut off the excess thread.

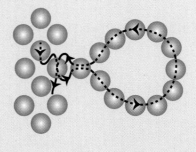

Figure 3

Step 5
Making the Bead End of the Clasp
Using the 12" tail of thread from the beginning of the first row, *PNT* the end beads until the thread comes out of the end bead of the middle row. String on two blue beads, one pink bead, the 10mm round glass luster bead with a rose, and one pink bead. *PNBT* the luster bead, one pink bead, and two blue beads. Weave thread through several stitches until secure and cut off the excess thread.

Step 6
Attaching the Center Dangle Bead
Using about 18" of thread, secure one end into choker by weaving it through several stitches until it comes out of the twenty-third end bead, next to the middle of the choker. String on one pink, the 18mm x 13mm luster bead, and one pink. *PNBT* the luster bead and the first pink bead. *PNT* the twenty-fourth end bead next to the middle of the choker and then weave in thread until secure and cut off excess thread.

RING

MATERIALS

28 light blue druk beads, 4mm
1 pink druk bead, 4mm
4 light green druk beads, 4mm
Nymo beading thread, size F, 1 yard

TOOLS

Beading needle, size 11

Step 1
Right Angle Weave Stitch

Using about 1 yard of thread, make four all-blue bead right-angle weave stitches. Make the next stitch using one green, one pink, one green. Then for the next stitch, string one green, one blue, one green. Make four more all-blue bead stitches.

Step 2
Making the Connecting Stitch

String one blue bead; *PNT* the end bead of the first stitch made. String one more blue bead, then *PNT* the end bead of the last stitch made, forming a circle (fig. 4). Weave end of thread back through stitches until secure. Cut off the excess.

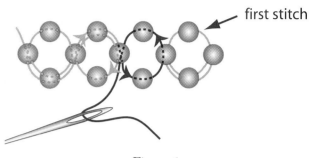

first stitch

Figure 4

6

Wirework Projects

This chapter skims the surface of all the things you can make with a little wire and beads. The basic techniques are few, but the possibilities are endless! The chapter has projects using memory wire, jump rings, head pins, eye pins, and chain.

Memory Wire
Choker and Ring

CHOKER

MATERIALS

1 loop of necklace memory wire, 14-1/2" long
6 gold AB bugle beads, 1/4"
12 white star beads, 5mm
4 light iris transparent teardrop beads, 5mm x 9mm
1 lantern-cut Swarovski crystal bead, 10mm
48 gold-lined seed beads, size 11°
72 light iris transparent triangle beads
2 crimp beads
2 gold clamshell bead tips

TOOLS

Crimp pliers
Flat-nose pliers
Flush style wire cutters

It is customary to end memory wire with a loop; however memory wire is very thick and it will bend most jewelers' round-nose pliers, so regular strength round-nose pliers must be used. We wanted to try something different, so we used a crimp bead and a bead tip to end the memory wire. You may use whichever technique you feel most comfortable with.

Step 1
Attaching the Crimp Bead and Bead Tip to the Memory Wire

Slip bead tip, then a crimp bead onto one end of the memory wire. Crimp the crimp bead, using the crimp pliers, onto the very end of the memory wire. Use wire cutters to trim off any excess wire sticking out of crimp bead. Now slip the bead tip up to and over the crimp bead to hide it. Squeeze bead tip closed over crimp bead. Wiggle hook end of the bead tip back and forth until it breaks off.

Step 2
Stringing the Beads

String beads onto the memory wire in this order: one gold seed bead, three triangle beads, one gold, one star bead, one gold, three triangles, one gold, one bugle bead, one gold, three triangles, one gold, one star, one gold, three triangles, one gold, one bugle, one gold, three triangles, one gold, one star, one gold, three triangles, one gold, one bugle, one gold, three triangle, one gold, one star, one gold, three triangles, one gold, one teardrop, one gold, three triangles, one gold, one star, one gold, three triangles, one gold, one teardrop, one gold, three triangles, one gold, one star, one gold, three triangles, one gold, one purple crystal. Repeat this pattern backwards for the other side of the choker. Finish the end with a crimp bead and a clamshell bead tip, repeating Step 1.

RING

MATERIALS

1 loop of ring memory wire, about 3-5/8" long
2 gold clamshell bead tips
2 crimp beads
4 white star beads
15 light iris transparent triangle beads
10 gold-lined seed beads, size 11°

TOOLS

Crimp pliers
Flat-nose pliers

Step 1
Attaching the Crimp Bead and the Bead Tip

Attach a crimp bead and bead tip to one end of the ring memory wire the same way as described in Step 1 of choker instructions.

Step 2
Stringing the Beads

String the beads onto the memory wire in this order: one gold seed bead, three triangle beads, one gold, one star, one gold, three triangles, one gold, one star, one gold, three triangles, one gold, one star, one gold, three triangles, one gold, one star, one gold, three triangles, one gold. Attach a crimp bead and bead tip to the end of the wire.

Wirework Rosebud Bracelet and Anklet

BRACELET

MATERIALS

11 transparent pink triangle beads, size 6°
22 transparent green seed beads, size 10°
12 jump rings (handmade or store bought; for hand
    made, see Techniques, page 24)
26-gauge silver wire, about 18″
1 silver hook-and-eye clasp

TOOLS

Round-nose pliers
Flat-nose pliers
Wire cutters

Step 1
Making the Wire and Bead Rosebuds

Cut a length of wire 1-1/2″ long. With round-nose
pliers grab one end of the wire, placing the wire about
1/8″ beyond the end of the pliers' nose and, using
your other hand, wrap the wire around the jaw of the
pliers forming a loop (fig. 1). Release the pliers from
the loop you just made and grab the wire just above
the loop and wrap the wire around the jaw of the pliers, moving the pliers up the wire as needed to form a
curve. Have the wire touch the loop after the curve
has been formed (fig. 2). Slip one green bead, one
pink bead and one green bead onto the wire end.
Make another loop and curve on the straight end of
the wire in the opposite direction of the first loop and
curve (fig. 3). Make 11 rosebuds (or enough to fit
your wrist).

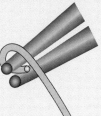

Figure 1

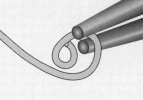

Figure 2

Figure 3

Step 2
Attaching the Rosebuds Together
Using jump rings, attach the rosebuds together. See
Techniques, page 24, on how to open and close a
jump ring (fig. 4).

Figure 4

Step 3
Attaching the Clasp
Use jump rings to attach the clasp to the ends of the
bracelet.

Use amber beads, the wrapped loop technique, and jump rings to create this lovely bracelet.

ANKLET

MATERIALS

15 transparent pink triangle beads, size 6°
30 transparent green seed beads, size 10°
*16 jump rings (handmade or store bought; for hand-
    made, see Techniques, page 24)*
20-gauge silver wire, about 24"
1 silver barrel clasp

TOOLS

Round-nose pliers
Flat-nose pliers
Wire cutters

Step 1
Making the Wire and Bead Rosebuds
Make the rosebuds the same way as the rosebuds in
the bracelet. Make 15 rosebuds (or enough to fit your
ankle). You could also make more to create a choker
or necklace.

Step 2
Attaching the Rosebuds Together
Use jump rings to attach the rosebuds together.

Step 3
Attaching the Clasp
Instructions for attaching the anklet clasp are the
same as the bracelet instructions.

Rhinestone Necklace and Earrings

NECKLACE

MATERIALS

2 two-ring rhinestone florets
5 three-ring rhinestone florets
5 clear glass faceted teardrop beads,
    9mm x 7mm
12" fancy gold cable chain (six 1" lengths
    and two 2" lengths)
5 gold head pins
1 gold hook and eye clasp
21 gold jump rings

TOOLS

Round nose pliers
Flat nose pliers
Wire cutters

Step 1
Cutting the Chain
Using the wire cutters, cut the chain into six 1"
lengths and two 2" lengths. Set aside.

Step 2
Making the Dangles
Place a teardrop bead on a head pin. With the flat
nose pliers, make a 90-degree angle in the wire close
to the bead. Cut the wire 1/4" from the bend. With
the round nose pliers, grab the end of the wire and,
with a turning motion, bend the end of the wire into
a loop. Repeat with the other four teardrop beads for
a total of five dangles.

Step 3
Attaching the Dangles to the Florets
Attach each dangle to a 3-ring floret using a jump
ring (fig. 1).

Figure 1

Step 4
Putting the Necklace Together

Attach one end of the clasp to one of the 2" chains using a jump ring. Attach the other end of the chain to a 2-ring floret, also using a jump ring (fig. 2). Use a jump ring to attach a 1" length of chain to the other ring of the 2-ring floret. *To the other end of the 1" chain attach (using a jump ring) a 3-ring floret with the dangle at the bottom (fig. 3). Make sure the florets are facing up. On the remaining open ring of the floret, attach another 1" chain using a jump ring.* Repeat between the asterisks four times. Now attach the remaining 2-ring floret to the 1" chain using a jump ring. Then attach the remaining 2" chain to the end of the 2-ring floret. And finally, using a jump ring, attach the other end of the clasp to the chain.

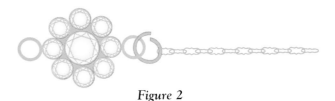

Figure 2

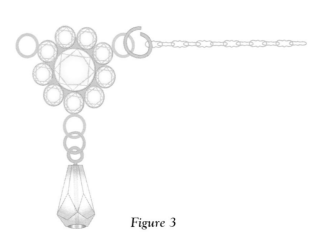

Figure 3

EARRINGS

MATERIALS

2 gold lever-back earring wires
2 two-ring rhinestone florets
2 gold head pins
2 gold jump rings
2 clear glass faceted teardrop beads, 9mm x 7mm

TOOLS

Flat-nose pliers
Round-nose pliers

Step 1
Making the Dangle

Place a teardrop bead on a head pin. Make a loop in the top of the head pin wire. See the technique section for detailed instructions. Attach the teardrop dangle onto one end of the 2-ring floret using a jump ring (fig. 4).

Figure 4

Step 2
Attaching the Earring Wire

Open the loop on the lever-back earring wire using the flat-nose pliers. Slip the loop into the ring on the floret opposite the teardrop bead. Close the loop with the pliers. Repeat Steps 1 and 2 for the other earring.

Carnelian Daisy and Chain Necklace and Earrings

This beautiful necklace was designed by Amy Gourley. She was inspired by jewelry worn in the Victorian age.

NECKLACE

MATERIALS

26-gauge gold wire, 7 feet
Figaro gold chain, 5 yards
1 gold fishhook clasp
2 fancy separator bars
15 gold jump rings
14 carnelian beads, 6mm
7 carnelian beads, 8mm
1 red glass drop bead, 1"

TOOLS

Side-style wire cutters
Chain-nose pliers
Round-nose pliers

Step 1
Making the Three Carnelian Daisies

First make the two small daisies. Use about 24" of the 26-gauge wire for each daisy. String six carnelian beads (6mm) onto the wire. Move the beads to the center of the wire. String the wire back through the first bead strung on forming a circle (fig. 1). String on one carnelian bead (6mm) and pass the wire through the fourth bead of the bead circle (this is a daisy chain stitch; see fig. 2).

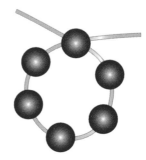

Figure 1

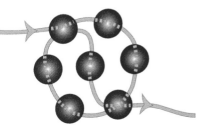

Figure 2

Make a wrapped loop (see Techniques, page 23, on how to make a wrapped loop) on each of the wire ends as close to the beads as possible (fig. 3).

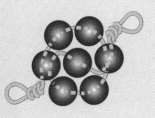

Figure 3

Now make the large daisy. Use about 36" of 26 gauge wire. Repeat the directions for the small daisies only use the 8mm carnelian beads. Make only one wrapped loop and on the other end of the wire just wrap it twice around the circle wire between the two beads. Cut excess wire. Use a jump ring to attach the drop bead to the wrapped loop. Now attach a jump ring between beads two and three, and one between beads four and five (fig. 4).

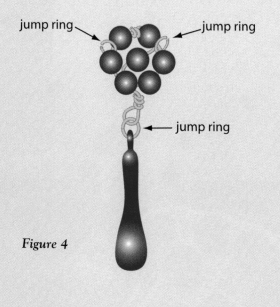

Figure 4

Step 2
Cutting the Chain and Attaching the Daisies

Cut four lengths of chain 3-1/4" long, four lengths of chain 3-1/2" long and four lengths of chain 4" long. Attach the chains with the short ones on top, medium ones in the middle and the long ones on the bottom. Use jump rings to attach the chain to all four of the wrapped loops on the small daisies and use the two jump rings already attached to the large daisy to attach the chains to the large daisy (fig. 5). Attach the end lengths of chain to the separator bars with jump rings (fig. 6). Make sure you keep the chains in the right order so they don't twist.

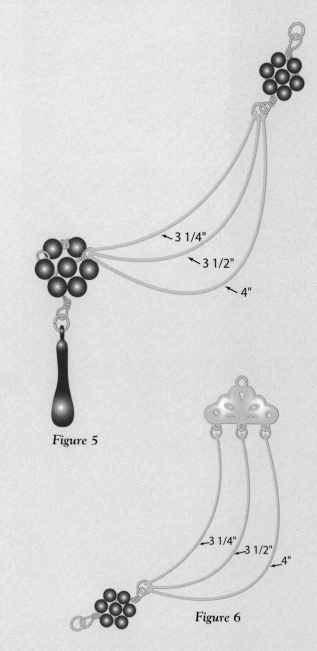

Figure 5

Figure 6

Step 3
Attaching the Clasp
Use jump rings to attach the clasp to the separator bars.

EARRINGS

MATERIALS

26-gauge gold wire, 14"
2 gold jump rings
2 red glass drop beads, 1"
2 carnelian beads, 8mm
2 gold fishhook ear wires

TOOLS

Round-nose pliers
Side style wire cutters

Step 1
Making the Dangle
Cut a 7" length of 26-gauge wire. String on one carnelian bead (8mm) and move the bead to the middle of the wire. Make a wrapped wire loop on each end as close to the bead as possible (fig. 7). Attach a red drop bead to one of the wrapped wire loops using a jump ring.

Figure 7

Step 2
Attaching the Ear Wire
Using round-nose pliers, open the loop on the end of the ear wire. Slip the wrapped loop that doesn't have the drop bead on it into the loop of the earring wire and close the loop with the round-nose pliers. Repeat Steps 1 and 2 for the other earring.

Red Glass Beads and Wire Necklace and Earrings

NECKLACE

MATERIALS

2 red faceted teardrop beads (with the hole running down through them), 7mm x 5mm

1 smooth red glass teardrop bead, 13mm x 8mm

24 round faceted glass beads in various shades of red to orange, 5mm

34 round faceted glass beads in various shades of red to orange, 4mm

52 round faceted glass beads in various shades of red to orange, 3mm

7 gold head pins, .025"

18 gold eye pins (you might want to get extras just in case), .021"

2 gold jump rings

1 lobster claw clasp

1 length of 24-gauge gold wire, 2"

TOOLS

Round-nose pliers

Flat-nose pliers

Wire cutters

Step 1
Making the Beaded Crescents

Use darker beads for the middle of the necklace and then use lighter and lighter beads as you get toward the back of the necklace. Place one of each of the following, in the sequence given, onto an eye pin: 3mm bead, 4mm bead, 5mm bead, 4mm bead, 3mm bead. Bend the end of the wire at a 90-degree angle using the flat-nose pliers as close to the beads as possible.

With the round-nose pliers, grab the wire as close to the bend as possible and wrap the wire around the jaw of the pliers to form a loop the same size as the eye pin loop. (The round-nose pliers are tapered, so find a place on the pliers that is the same circumference as the eyelet on the eye pin and make the loops at this same spot every time—or you could use coil pliers.) Slide another eye pin into the loop you just made and cut the excess wire from the loop and close the loop with pliers (fig. 1). Using your fingers, bend the eye pin with the beads on it into a crescent

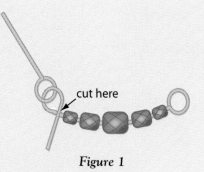

cut here

Figure 1

shape. Continue in this manner until you have eight beaded crescent shaped eye pins. Don't close the loop of the last crescent; set aside. Now make one more chain of eight beaded crescent shaped eye pins. Remember to leave the loop open on the last crescent.

Step 2
Making the Dangles

To make the center dangle place the 13mm smooth teardrop, and one round 15mm bead onto a head pin and then form a loop and close it. (See Techniques, page 23.) Set aside and then make the two side dangles. Place a 7mm faceted teardrop bead and three round 3mm beads on a head pin, form a loop, but leave it open. Make one more. Set aside. There are four more dangles: Two with one 5mm bead and two 3mm beads on a head pin and two dangles with one 5mm bead and one 3mm bead on a head pin. Make the loops on these four, but don't close them. Set aside.

Step 3
Making the Center Double Crescent

To make the center double crescent, attach an eye pin to the open eyelet end of one of the eight crescent chains. Also on this eye pin, attach one of the four bead faceted teardrop side dangles. Close the loops and make sure the dangle is attached under the crescent (fig. 2). At the straight end of the eye pin

attach a length of 24-gauge wire about 2" long by twisting the 24-gauge wire twice around the eye pin. Clip any excess wire (fig. 3). On the eye pin, place three 3mm beads, one 5mm bead, the center dangle with the smooth teardrop bead, one 5mm bead, and three 3mm beads. Form the beaded eye pin into a crescent, being careful not to let the beads slip off the end of the eye pin. Take the 24-gauge wire and put on one 3mm bead, one 4mm bead, one 5mm bead, one 4mm bead, and one 3mm bead. Now wrap the end of the 24-gauge wire twice around the eye pin just above the beads. Cut the excess 24-gauge wire and in the eye pin make a loop right above the wrapped 24-gauge wire. Close the loop. Now slip the open loop of the other four bead faceted teardrop dangle into the eye pin loop just made, and then slip the open loop of the other eight crescent chain onto the eye pin loop just made and close the loops.

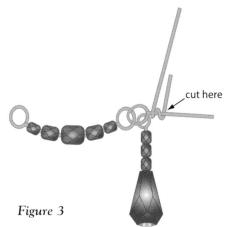

Figure 3

Step 4
Adding the Four Small Side Dangles

Attach the three bead dangles on the crescents on either side of the center double crescent. Attach the two bead dangles on the crescents on either side of the three bead dangles (fig. 4).

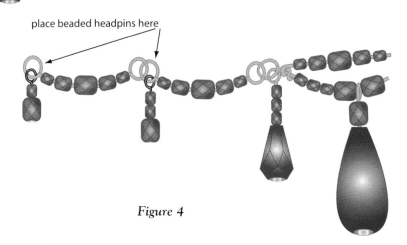

Figure 2

Figure 4

Step 5
Attaching the Clasp

Put jump rings on each end of the necklace and attach the lobster claw clasp to the jump rings.

EARRINGS

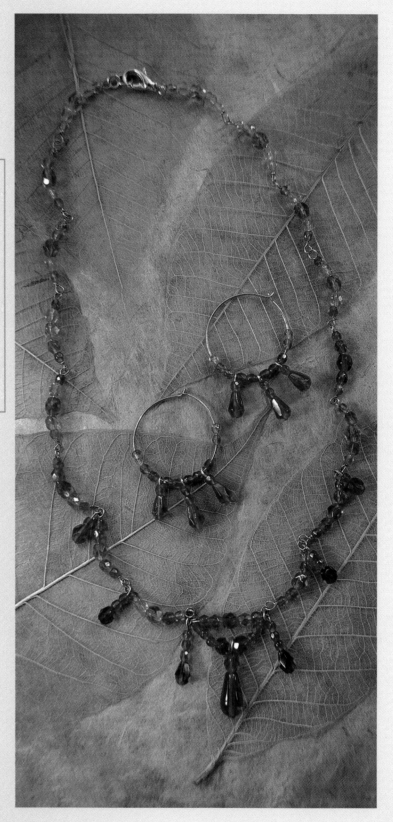

MATERIALS

6 red faceted teardrop beads (with the hole running down through it), 7mm x 5mm
28 round faceted glass beads in various shades of red to orange, 3mm
6 gold head pins, .025"
2 gold hoop earring wires

TOOLS

Round-nose pliers
Flat-nose pliers
Wire cutters

Step 1
Making the Dangles

Place one teardrop bead and one 3mm bead onto a head pin. Form a loop on the head pin as close to the beads as possible, cut excess wire, and close the loop with pliers. Make two. For the middle dangle, place one teardrop bead and two 3mm beads onto a head pin and form a loop, cut excess wire and close the loop.

Step 2
Stringing the Beads

Onto one of the hoop earring wires, string three 3mm beads, one two-bead dangle, two 3mm beads, one three-bead dangle, two 3mm beads, one two-bead dangle and three 3mm beads. Bend the end of the hoop up at a 90-degree angle so it will fit into the hole on the other end of the hoop. Repeat for the other earring.

Jump Ring Netted
Necklace and Bracelet

This necklace is composed of 53 beaded eye pins connected by jump rings.

NECKLACE

MATERIALS

53 matte metallic olive green seed beads, size 6°
106 dark metallic with bronze finish seed beads, size 10°
5 black metallic luster finished faceted teardrop beads, 7mm x 5mm
42 gold jump rings, 5mm
53 gold eye pins
5 gold head pins
1 gold lobster claw clasp

TOOLS

Round-nose pliers
Flat-nose pliers
Chain-nose pliers
Wire cutters

Step 1
Making the Beaded Eye Pins

Slip one size 10° seed bead, one size 6° seed bead and one size 10° seed bead onto an eye pin. Using the flat-nose pliers, bend the straight wire above the beads at a 90-degree angle. Next, make a loop as follows: With the round-nose pliers, hold the wire as close to the bend as possible and, with your fingers or the chain-nose pliers, bend the wire around the top jaw of the pliers, pulling tight (fig. 1). Make sure the loop is the same size as the eyelet on the other side. Cut the excess wire and close the loop with round-nose pliers. (Determine where on the round-nose pliers it is the same diameter as the eyelet on the eye pin, and wrap the wire around the same spot every time you make a loop.) Make 53.

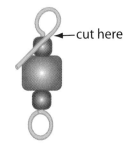
cut here

Figure 1

Step 2
Constructing the Main Chain of the Necklace

Open a jump ring (see Techniques, page 24, for how to open and close a jump ring), and slip the loops from two beaded eye pins onto the jump ring. Close the jump ring. Now open another jump ring and slip it onto the other loop of one of the attached beaded eye pins. Pick up another beaded eye pin and slip one of its loops onto this jump ring also. Close the jump ring (fig. 2). Continue adding a beaded eye pin to the chain until you have eleven attached beaded eye pins. To one end of the chain attach a jump ring and two beaded eye pins. Close the jump ring. Allow the first beaded eye pin to dangle and the other eye pin will be used for the main chain. Attach a jump ring with three beaded eye pins to the empty loop of the eye pin that isn't dangling (the main chain one). Close the jump ring. Allow the first two beaded eye pins to dangle and use the third one as the main chain (fig. 3). * Attach a jump ring with three beaded eye pins to the empty loop of the main chain eye pin. Allow two beaded eye pins to dangle and use the third one as the main chain eye pin.* Repeat between asterisks four more times. Next add two beaded eye pins to a jump ring and the jump ring to the main chain eye pin. Allow one eye pin to dangle like the one at the beginning and use the other one as the main chain. To this main chain eye pin attach, with jump rings, 11 more beaded eye pins. The main chain is now finished.

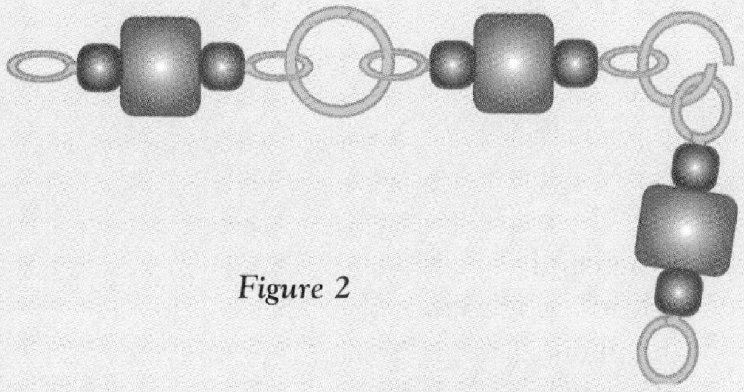

Figure 2

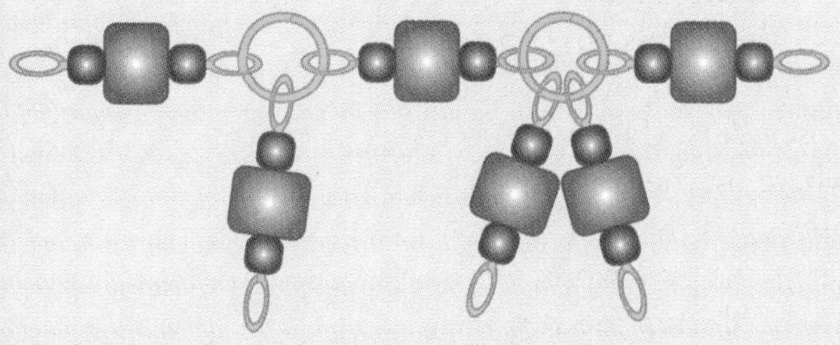

Figure 3

Step 3
Making the Five Teardrop Dangles

Put a teardrop bead onto a head pin and make a loop at the end as close to the top of the bead as possible. Make five and set aside.

Step 4
Row Two

Open a jump ring and place one of the teardrop dangles onto it. Connect the first two dangling beaded eye pins on the main chain with the jump ring with the teardrop dangle on it. Close the jump ring. Open another jump ring and slip a beaded eye pin onto it. Connect the next two dangling beaded eye pins with this jump ring (fig. 4). * Open another jump ring and slip two beaded eye pins onto it and then use this jump ring to connect the next two eye pins dangling from the main chain. Close the jump ring.* Repeat between asterisks twice. Then open another jump ring and slip on one beaded eye pin; use this jump ring to attach the next two beaded eye pins dangling from the main chain. Close the jump ring. Open another jump ring and slip one of the teardrop dangles onto it and use this jump ring to connect the last two beaded eye pins dangling from the main chain. Close the jump ring.

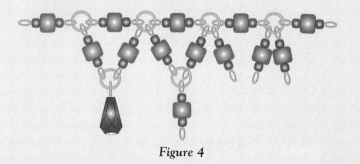

Figure 4

Step 5
Row Three

Open a jump ring and slip one of the teardrop dangles onto it, then use this jump ring to connect the first two dangling beaded eye pins from Row 2. Close the jump ring. * Open another jump ring and slip on one beaded eye pin, and use this jump ring to connect the next two dangling beaded eye pins from Row 2. Close the jump ring. * Repeat between asterisks once. To connect the last two beaded eye pins dangling from Row 3, use a jump ring with a teardrop dangle on it.

Step 6
Row Four

Open a jump ring and slip on the last teardrop dangle. Use this jump ring to connect the two dangling beaded eye pins from Row 3. Close the jump ring.

Step 7
Attaching the Clasp

Attach the clasp ends to each end of the necklace using jump rings.

BRACELET

MATERIALS

14 matte metallic olive green seed beads, size 6°
28 metallic dark with bronze tinge seed beads, size 10°
5 black metallic luster finished faceted teardrop beads, 7mm x 5mm
15 gold jump rings, 5mm
14 gold eye pins
5 gold head pins
1 gold lobster claw clasp

TOOLS

Round-nose pliers
Flat-nose pliers
Chain-nose pliers
Wire cutters

Step 1
Making the Beaded Eye Pins and the Five Teardrop Dangles

Make 14 beaded eye pins the same way as in Step 1 of the necklace. Make five teardrop dangles the same way as in Step 3 of the necklace.

Step 2
Making a Beaded Eye Pin Chain

Using jump rings, make a chain with three beaded eye pins.

Step 3
Constructing the Bracelet

* Put a teardrop dangle and a beaded eye pin onto a jump ring. Connect this jump ring to the three beaded eye pin chain. Let the teardrop dangle, then on the beaded eye pin attach another eye pin with a jump ring * (fig. 5). Repeat between the asterisks four times then add one more beaded eye pin.

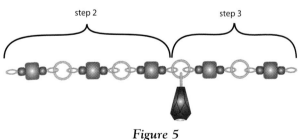

step 2   step 3

Figure 5

Step 4
Attaching the Clasp

Attach the clasp ends to each end of the bracelet using jump rings.

Resource List

Fire Mountain Gems
#1 Fire Mountain Wy., Dept. F036
Grants Pass, OR 97526-2373
(800) 423-2319 INFO
(800) 355-2137 ORDER
(800) 292-3473 FAX
www.firemountaingems.com

General Bead
317 National City Blvd.
National City, CA 91950
(619) 336-0100
(800) 572-1302 FAX
www.genbead.com

Creative Castle
2321 Michael Dr.
Newbury Park, CA 91320
(805) 499-1377
www.creativecastle.com

Kandra's Beads
570 Higuera St., Ste #125
San Luis Obispo, CA 93401
(800) 454-7079
www.kandrasbeads.com

Index